Constructing Student Mobility

Constructing Student Mobility

How Universities Recruit Students and Shape Pathways
between Berkeley and Seoul

Stephanie K. Kim

The MIT Press

Cambridge, Massachusetts | London, England

The MIT Press would like to thank the anonymous peer reviewers who provided comments on drafts of this book. The generous work of academic experts is essential for establishing the authority and quality of our publications. We acknowledge with gratitude the contributions of these otherwise uncredited readers.

This book was set in Stone Serif by Westchester Publishing Services. Printed and bound in the United States of America.

Library of Congress Cataloging-in-Publication Data

Names: Kim, Stephanie K., author.
Title: Constructing student mobility : how universities recruit students
    and shape pathways between Berkeley and Seoul / Stephanie K. Kim.
Description: Cambridge, Massachusetts : The MIT Press, 2023. | Includes
    bibliographical references and index.
Identifiers: LCCN 2022028460 (print) | LCCN 2022028461 (ebook) |
    ISBN 9780262545143 (paperback) | ISBN 9780262373388 (epub) |
    ISBN 9780262373371 (pdf)
Subjects: LCSH: College student mobility—California. | College student
    mobility—Korea (South) | College students—Recruiting—California. |
    College students—Recruiting—Korea (South) | University of California,
    Berkeley—Admission. | Yŏnse Taehakkyo—Admission. |
    College students—Korea (South)
Classification: LCC LA230 .K56 2023 (print) | LCC LA230 (ebook) |
    DDC 378.1/61—dc23/eng/20220722
LC record available at https://lccn.loc.gov/2022028460
LC ebook record available at https://lccn.loc.gov/2022028461

10 9 8 7 6 5 4 3 2 1

For Jack

Contents

Author's Note ix

Acknowledgments xi

1 "Those Rich International Students" 1
2 A Pathway into UC Berkeley 27
3 A Pathway into Yonsei University 57
4 The Contradictions of Choice 87
5 The Global Student Supply Chain 119
6 Lessons from a Turbulent Decade 157

Methodological Appendix 175

Notes 181

Bibliography 191

Index 205

Author's Note

I follow the Revised Romanization system for the romanization of Korean words. When writing names, I use the Korean name convention of family name first followed by the given name, without the use of a hyphen. Exceptions are made for individuals who have clearly indicated a preferred spelling or name order, for names of public figures with a commonly recognized English transliteration, for official names of institutions, and for the surnames Kim and Lee. Additionally, I use pseudonyms to represent any individuals interviewed for this book.

Significant portions of chapter 3 were published as a journal article in the *Journal of Korean Studies*. Duke University Press provided permission to reprint the material.

Acknowledgments

Where do I begin? Most immediately, I want to thank the students who shared their stories with me so that I may include them here, as well as many other individuals who shared their time and expertise with grace and patience. Though I cannot name you directly, do know that I am incredibly grateful for your gift. Without you, this book would not be possible.

I also want to thank everyone who played a direct role in the book's publication. I'm indebted to Jenny Lee, Jiyeon Kang, Yingyi Ma, Chris Glass, and Phan Le Ha for giving extensive feedback on earlier drafts. The anonymous peer reviewers also gave a helpful balance of sharp and encouraging commentary that motivated me to make this book the best possible version that I could. It goes without saying that the publication of the book would not have been possible without the support of my editor at the MIT Press, Susan Buckley, who I'm thankful for seeing the potential in my project and taking a chance on this first-time book author. Claire Catenaccio helped give the manuscript its final polish with her keen editorial eye. And a hearty thank you goes to Carole Sargent, whose unorthodox yet highly effective advice was instrumental in shepherding me through the publication process.

The ideas in this book are inspired by the work of many scholars, and I hope I have done justice to their work through my engagement with it. I'm lucky to call some of these great minds my friends and colleagues. I'm especially fortunate to have brilliant scholars like Hyungryeol Kim, Christina Yao, and Jae-Eun Jon in my life. Your support and encouragement helped me get this book over the finish line. You also make conferencing so fun! I also want to thank my colleagues across Georgetown University, especially those in the School of Continuing Studies, Asian Studies Program, and Education Working Group, who were enthusiastic cheerleaders throughout this process.

Several organizations provided support for the book. Grants from the Korea Foundation, Association for Asian Studies, and Fulbright program funded my research. Additional grants from Georgetown University made possible the last stages of my research, as did support from Kelly Otter and Shenita Ray in the School of Continuing Studies. The George Washington Institute for Korean Studies hosted a book manuscript workshop for me, and I thank Jisoo Kim and Immanuel Kim for supporting this. The Social Science Research Council allowed me to participate in a Korean studies workshop for junior faculty that helped me shape my nascent ideas into a doable project. The seasoned discussants Suzy Kim, Seungsook Moon, and Jenny Gavacs made the book publication process less opaque, while Nicole Restrick Levit and my workshop compatriots made a long weekend in Upstate New York a truly enjoyable experience. I also benefited tremendously as a Center for Strategic and International Studies U.S.-Korea Next-Gen Scholar. The sage mentoring by Victor Cha and David Kang, and the supportive community from my fellow NextGen Scholars, were instrumental to my professional development.

Numerous people whom I encountered at UC Berkeley made a mark on this book in some fashion. I especially thank John Lie, Laura Nelson, and Jinsoo An, who were steadfast in seeing me develop as a scholar. Of course, I could not have gotten anything done at the Center for Korean Studies without Clare You, Dianne Enpa-Cho, Yu

Jung Kim, Yoojin Lee, and Rosa Kwak. My colleagues across the Institute of East Asian Studies were invaluable sources of knowledge as I turned to them with my many questions. My patient tutor, Yoonmi Woo, helped me improve my Korean to a more professional level that benefitted the research for this book. I also thank the many scholars who passed through the Center and the Institute when I coordinated their talks, and the regular participants of the biweekly Korean studies seminars—your work certainly sparked my own creativity. And I'm grateful to have been looped into the various projects and events at the Center for Studies in Higher Education.

A number of people at Yonsei University also contributed to the making of this book. I'm thankful to the faculty members and administrators who shared their time and expertise with me, especially when I was just a graduate student going about her dissertation research who had no idea what kind of trajectory my project would take. And I would be remiss not to mention that my year living and conducting research in Seoul was made possible by support from Fulbright Korea, its former executive director Jai Ok Shim, and my community of Fulbright researchers.

Many organizations provided a platform where I could share my work and cultivate my ideas, including the *Journal of International Students*, Korea Economic Institute, USC Korean Studies Institute, Penn James Joo-Jin Kim Center for Korean Studies, Stanford Shorenstein Asia-Pacific Research Center, Seoul National University Asia Center, East-West Center, Cal Tech Critical Intersections, President's Alliance on Higher Education and Immigration, New England Board of Higher Education, and Fulbright Association National Capital Area Chapter.

Writing this book coincided with a particularly challenging time in my life, not to mention a global pandemic. I was only able to finish it with support from my family, my partner, and our two mischievous critters. This book is dedicated to them.

1

"Those Rich International Students"

This book begins at the University of California, Berkeley, where I worked at the Center for Korean Studies for several years following the completion of my doctoral degree. One semester, I was invited to deliver a guest lecture in a Korean studies class on the significance of education to broader societal issues in South Korea. It was a topic I knew very well—I had written an entire dissertation on it—but I only knew it from an outsider's perspective, as an American studying the South Korean education system as an object of analysis. By contrast, the class was composed mostly of international students from South Korea who had come up through this very system and knew it intimately.

I gave a lecture on the extreme competition in the South Korean education system, a topic that I thought would resonate. After the lecture, students shared personal stories of intense test preparation regimes, grueling hours studying outside of normal school hours at hagwons, and in some cases, years spent living abroad separated from their family so that they could learn English. Always one to push the class discussion a little further, I asked the students a pointed question: "Did these experiences help you get into UC Berkeley?" The class went quiet until a particularly outspoken student named Sora piped up. Sora described how hard she had worked to excel in her studies, which, in her opinion, didn't just help her enter but, in fact, allowed her to *earn* her place at one of the most renowned universities in California. I asked what differentiated her from any other international student who presumably also earned her place. She retorted, "I'm not one of those rich international students." Her classmates nodded in agreement.

"Those rich international students" certainly hold their place in the American imagination. Films such as 2018's *Crazy Rich Asians* or salacious news articles about the children of royal sheiks depict international students as the nouveau riche who come from Asia or the Middle East. They bring their lavish lifestyles and tuition dollars to the United States because they are attracted to a liberal education absent in their so-called illiberal home countries. Scholars, too, have contributed to this imagination. In the groundbreaking book *Flexible Citizenship*, first published in 1999, the anthropologist Aihwa Ong gave us a new understanding of globalization as a horizonal movement, called transnationalism, that is practiced by exceptionally affluent and internationally mobile individuals. Ong developed these insights while observing the residents of Hong Kong who moved their finances overseas and obtained multiple passports as sovereignty over Hong Kong changed from British to Chinese rule. These flexible citizens are individuals who constantly reposition their citizenship (or citizenships) as a proactive strategy to accumulate more wealth and power in the context of global capitalism.

Flexible citizenship also goes hand in hand with global higher education, as affluent and mobile individuals seek academic credentials from universities that are themselves repositioning their global standing and preparing a highly skilled professional class for a globalized world.[1] And these individuals certainly bring dividends to the universities in which they enroll. Just prior to the COVID-19 pandemic, the 1.1 million international students enrolled in the American higher education sector in the 2019–2020 academic year contributed over $38 billion to the American economy.[2] This astronomical figure is in large part what fuels universities to increase international student enrollments, especially at public institutions facing declining state budgets that in turn look to international students as a financial panacea. In California, for example, the state that hosts by far the most international students, the 160,000 international students enrolled across California colleges and universities just prior to the pandemic contributed over $6.6 billion to the California economy.[3]

In fact, Aihwa Ong claimed to see these elite and empowered flexible citizens all over UC Berkeley, where we both worked. Yet Sora, the student who bristled at my question, certainly did not consider herself to be one despite that she seemingly fit the description. Sora described herself as an international student from South Korea who participated in what many other South Korean millennials had in their educational endeavors. She spent two years of elementary school in the United States for early study abroad, then returned to South Korea to complete middle and high school. She attended an international high school in Seoul, where the instruction was in English, before studying abroad once again as a college student. Yet she clearly reacted negatively to the implication that her college admission was related to her worldly background. By referring to "those rich international students" as a different campus demographic, she was able to fashion another kind of identity that downplayed her mobility and played up her credibility, by "earning" her spot at UC Berkeley.

Sora's reaction shows how even international students grapple with particular notions about themselves. While they may be flexible citizens, their everyday experiences on campus are clearly in tension with their assumed privilege. This is a direct result of the student recruitment efforts of the universities that they attend. Indeed, working from the assumption that they must compete for these affluent and mobile students, universities adopt reforms to attract these well-paying customers. So how, exactly, do universities do this? What brings students like Sora to a particular campus? And what actually happens to "those rich international students" once they arrive? My search for those answers began with this small encounter and expanded into a multiyear project spanning two continents and dozens of interlocutors. I began this research in Berkeley, revised my previous doctoral research conducted in Seoul, expanded the project to other parts of California, returned multiple times to South Korea, and eventually brought in insights from the policy world of Washington, DC.

Hence, this book takes an unusual turn in the scholarship on international student mobility. It centers on universities—rather than students—as the most important actors in understanding student mobility flows. Most studies on international student mobility focus on how students partake in global processes by pursuing education overseas.[4] Others show how higher education sectors merely respond to students going overseas in side-by-side country case studies.[5] By contrast, this book positions universities as the primary unit of analysis while also carefully tracing the individual and international relations within which this intermediary scale operates.[6]

Specifically, it presents two universities, one in Berkeley and the other in Seoul, that aggressively grew their student pools in the 2010s, a decade when international student recruitment became essential to the financial health of many higher education institutions. This book positions these universities as interconnected nodes by interrogating how each navigated challenging financial conditions through its student recruitment efforts. These universities are geographically, culturally, and linguistically miles apart, but they sought out students in similarly market-driven ways that configured and reconfigured student mobility flows across seemingly disparate higher education contexts. This book puts those contexts into conversation.

This book also challenges a flat view of internationally mobile students as wealthy and footloose. It offers an intimate and complicated portrayal of students from South Korea whose global aspirations are capitalized upon by the universities that they attend. It situates their experiences within their campus environment and shows how their lives are bound to the institutional configurations of higher education. These students may have been presented with the choice to pursue higher learning in one country or another, but the choice was often mediated by universities' financial realities. This book calls into question international student mobility as a privileged choice for privileged individuals.

Additionally, this book illuminates an expansive ecosystem of global higher education beyond universities. Indeed, students' choices to pursue higher learning are mediated by many other stakeholders that also capitalize on students' global aspirations. Unlike universities, they may not generate the actual opportunities for higher learning, but they facilitate the choices that students make and the pathways that they take while profiting from them. This book pays heed to the individual and institutional actors beyond universities that further shape student mobility flows around the world.

Constructing Student Mobility, therefore, argues that universities themselves shape the pathways that allow students their international mobility. They do so by rearranging their configurations to capitalize on students' global aspirations in their own pursuit of profit and prestige. This presents an unorthodox way of understanding student mobility flows that has implications for how scholars and practitioners alike can engage with the complex infrastructure of global higher education.

In this opening chapter, I introduce two distinct higher education contexts, California and South Korea, where one sees notably large numbers of inbound students, and the other sees notably large numbers of outbound students. I first situate student mobility flows between these particular scales because higher education policy and funding largely operate at the state level in the United States and at the national level in South Korea, before I delve into the institutional particularities of specific universities in Berkeley and Seoul in later chapters. I also present a different theoretical terrain to untangle the ebb and flow of students between these locales: that of flexible universities.

Contested Globalism in California

It was brisk fall evening when I attended a University of California alumni event to listen to former UC President Janet Napolitano speak about upcoming challenges to the California higher education sector. In a crowded conference room full of UC alums, a middle-aged White woman asked Napolitano why the UC system keeps accepting more international students and displacing in-state students from coveted seats. Napolitano responded with a financial argument: in fact, she explained, accepting more international students into the UC system actually increases the university's ability to accept more in-state students, because the higher tuition that international students pay subsidizes the tuition of California residents.

Public colleges and universities often tout this economic rationale to defend their growing proportion of international students. But until the Great Recession from 2007 to 2009, international students hardly amounted to single-digit proportions at most California institutions and, in fact, across most American institutions. While research universities did actively recruit international students as sources of talent within doctoral programs, particularly in the STEM fields, the turn to international undergraduate students—the majority of whom fund their studies from personal and family sources—did not happen until the last decade.[7] In 2000, for instance, the number of international undergraduate students enrolled across all of the UC campuses combined was slightly over 2,500, representing just 1.8 percent of total undergraduate student enrollment in the UC system (see figure 1.1).

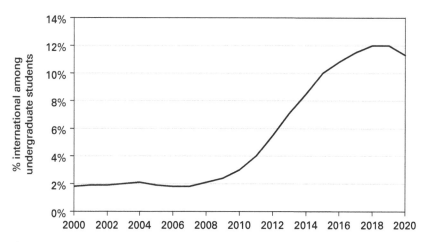

Figure 1.1
Proportion of international undergraduate students in the UC system, 2000–2020.
Source: UCOP, "Fall Enrollment at a Glance."

Indeed, the California higher education system was designed with a decidedly domestic purpose. The 1960 California Master Plan for Higher Education coordinated the University of California, California State University, and California Community Colleges into a single system that would provide high-quality, low-cost tertiary education for California's growing population. This system was born out of a larger movement in the United States to increase higher education access, affordability, and participation for Americans in the decades following World War II, what the higher education scholar John Thelin calls American higher education's Golden Age.[8] But after the Great Recession, higher education institutions sought out international students for revenue generation rather than talent acquisition. As a result, international student enrollment growth at the undergraduate level outpaced growth at the graduate level. In California, the 2009 state budget cuts led to California colleges and universities accepting more international undergraduate students in order to make up for the loss in state funds. And this California story became a recurring one across the United States as public colleges and universities in all fifty states faced similar financial pressures.

The conflation of international students with revenue generation is part of a broader turn toward market-driven logic in higher education, a trend for which the higher education scholars Sheila Slaughter and Larry Leslie coined the term "academic capitalism" in 1999.[9] Academic capitalism subverts the American ideal of higher learning as a public good and instead positions it as a private commodity to be bought and sold by providers (colleges and universities) to customers (students and their parents).[10] Academic capitalism provides an overarching framework through which we can understand other waves of critical scholarship in higher education that have emerged since the 1990s, which address the corporatization of universities alongside the exploitation of academic labor and the steep rise of tuition and student debt. This framework suggests that universities are no longer mainstays of knowledge production for the common good but market-driven institutions that mirror the values and activities of the global economy.

The alignment of higher education with the global economy began in 1995 when the World Trade Organization declared "educational services" a tradable commodity, a point that still evokes vehement debate among educationists with every new round of negotiations of the General Agreement on Trade in Services. In tandem with the rise of global rankings that pit institutions in different countries against one another, universities have reprioritized their activities in line with the buying and selling of their "services" across the world.[11] Scholars have explained this spectacular transformation of higher education sectors all over the world by pointing repeatedly to the same dynamic: that higher education institutions respond to an exogenous phenomenon called globalization, what Philip Altbach and Jane Knight have defined as "the economic, political, and societal forces pushing 21st century higher education toward greater international involvement."[12] Their definition parallels earlier sociological scholarship that uses institutional theory as a guiding framework to situate organizations within larger economic, political, and social environments, causing them to respond in homogenous and diverse ways.[13]

This particular framing of a global higher education system has influenced how scholars of higher education understand the relationship between globalization and the university, spurring over a decade of empirical studies that follow this particular methodology.[14] Within this understanding of global higher education, globalization touches all aspects of higher education, and universities all over the world are undertaking internationalization strategies in response. Jane Knight argues that the internationalization of higher education entails developing a set of rationales and outcomes in response to an externally global environment.[15] And as universities respond to globalization in increasingly market-driven ways, Nelly Stromquist argues that internationalization is first and foremost concerned with a search for more students.[16] Internationalization, then, is widely understood as the institutional response to what we can aptly call global student markets.[17] As students become more internationally mobile and pursue higher education overseas as a part of participating in the global economy, scholars argue that universities respond to this new reality by adopting internationalization reforms that will attract these students, sometimes strategically and sometimes reactively. In short, the mobile trajectories of students have been treated as the given context against which universities must adapt.

Just as the United States dominates the global economy, American higher education dominates global student markets, in large part due to the sector's supremacy in global rankings.[18] But in recent years, growing nativist sentiment and the changing political milieu in the United States have dampened new international student enrollment. In particular, the Trump administration aggressively policed the influx of new entrants into the country under the banner of restoring the United States to its past glory, largely imagined, through draconian immigration policies.[19] Nativist rhetoric and action then expanded into the higher education sector with policies that restricted international students from coming to or staying in the United States.[20] Racialized portrayals of COVID-19 as the "Chinese virus" and deteriorating relations between the United States and China have further contributed to antagonism toward international students, especially those from Asian countries.[21] This unwelcome climate has had real effects: new international student enrollment in the United States decreased annually since 2016 even before it plummeted in 2020.[22]

It is against this politically charged backdrop that pundits have begun to point out how American higher education, once unparalleled in its ability to attract international students, is now losing its global edge.[23] These same pundits point to Canada or Australia, which recently appear to be a more attractive destination for international students compared to a seemingly hostile United States. This anxiety over lost tuition and talent hinges on the assumption that American exceptionalism has eroded and that this erosion now affects the politics of higher education. Whether or not this picture is accurate—after all, the United States is still by far host to the largest number of international students—universities across the United States are now much more conscious of their global standing and much less inclined to take international student enrollment for granted.

The perception that American higher education must now compete on the global stage certainly affects how the California higher education system attracts international students. Across the spectrum of the state's research universities to the community colleges, California higher education institutions have set up special functions that cater to and profit from international students. These range from the creation of international student services to the hiring of admissions recruiters to the incorporation of bridge programs that all work to recruit and retain international students, who are no longer considered an endless stream of revenue but a finite source to be mined. But there is also growing discontent in California over how the state's resources seem to prioritize international students at the expense of domestic students. The very fact that Janet Napolitano expected a question at a UC alumni event about international students displacing in-state students in California speaks to this brewing tension.

This domestic pushback has made college admissions a hotly contested arena where issues of access, equity, racism, and xenophobia collide, with international students standing at the center of these tensions. Nonetheless, as Napolitano's answer shows, the California higher education system as a whole continues to facilitate entryways for international students, even as individual institutions may cave to domestic pressure and restrict access. These competing pressures create novel admissions pathways for international students. And a noticeably large proportion of those international students who enter into them come from South Korea.

A Different Globalism in South Korea

"1, 2, 3, 4, 5 . . ." A young woman strikes a hammer over a three-inch steel cube shaped like a house, counting out loud with each strike. When she reaches one hundred, she folds a piece of paper into the shape of a tiny house and places it gently beside her on the floor. She repeats this act over and over until she is surrounded by tiny paper houses, while the steel house wears down into a dull nub. This repetitive act by South Korean artist Minji Sohn was a performance piece titled "Lost Homes" that was part of her "1, 2, 3, 4, 5 . . . 100" exhibition shown through the Minnesota Street Project in San Francisco in 2015. While critics interpreted this piece as a somber take on displacement and relocation caused by the San Francisco Bay Area housing crisis, Sohn herself has said that it also reflects her own life as a "foreign student moving from country to country and city to city" apart from her family since the age of eleven.[24] Sohn left South Korea for Toronto, then Chicago, then New York, then the Bay Area, to attain advanced schooling and English fluency. Her provocative performance piece speaks to this constant movement and the elusiveness of home.

Sohn's performance piece is unique, but her personal story is actually quite ordinary among South Koreans. Indeed, the callous ordinariness of South Korean youth sent overseas en masse to attend school in English-speaking countries is exactly what propelled the themes in Sohn's art. After Sohn finished the sixth grade in South Korea, she attended a boarding school in Canada, where she lived nine months out of the year "in a foreign land speaking a foreign language" and the other three months with her family in South Korea over summer breaks. Like Sohn, for at least the last several decades many South Korean youth from upper- and middle-class backgrounds were sent overseas for early study abroad, and this transnational experience has markedly shaped the South Korean millennial's childhood.[25] These youngsters left South Korea to attend school in English-speaking countries along the Pacific Rim, such as the United States, Canada, Australia, and New Zealand, and later Singapore and the Philippines. Often the father remained at home in South Korea and sent the bulk of his earnings to his wife and child, who lived overseas so that the child could attain English fluency and the mother could manage the child's education. Since the mid-1990s, such transnational families engaged in overseas sojourns mostly during the child's middle and high school years, but since the early 2000s, they were increasingly characterized by early study abroad during the child's elementary school years. The zeal for English language education and the highly competitive South Korean education system created a transnational family network of financial and emotional sacrifice, often in the form of split families, in pursuit of the child's accumulation of global cultural capital.[26]

These factors are what make South Koreans of the millennial generation an important analytic category through which we can investigate questions of student mobility. While migration studies traditionally frame the movement of people through economic and political lenses, recently scholars have turned to an education lens as a way to understand mobility, particularly through the concept of aspiration, as individuals move from east to west, or south to north, in pursuit of higher learning and world-class credentials.[27] The concept of aspiration implicitly centers on the individual, imbuing each person with agency and subjectivity. So Jin Park and Nancy Abelmann call this "cosmopolitan striving" on the part of South Korean youth and their managerial parents that intersects with dominant ideologies of English and neoliberalism.[28] The fruits of overseas study and English fluency are then realized via the local benefits (e.g., academic achievement, job market success) within South Korea.[29]

It is unsurprising, then, to see South Korea rank so highly among top contributors of international students to American higher education. For the last two decades, South Korea has been consistently the third largest contributor of international students to the United States after China and India (see table 1.1). This is an amazing feat, considering that China and India each have a population of over 1.3 billion, which dwarfs South Korea's 51 million. Just prior to the pandemic, students from South Korea enrolled in US colleges and universities in the 2019–2020 academic year totaled nearly 50,000.[30] When adjusted for population, South Korea contributed over three times more students than China and over six times more students than India to the American higher education sector. Notably, the South Korean government does not provide financial assistance to its students who study abroad; such endeavors are pursued and financed privately by students and their families, reflecting the country's broad demand for overseas higher education, and indeed, higher education more generally. South Korea boasts of the world's highest overall rate of youth who attain higher education.

The flipside to these impressive numbers is that the South Korean higher education sector has been struggling because of the

Table 1.1
Leading places of origin of international students in US higher education, 2000–2020

2000–2001	2005–2006	2010–2011	2015–2016	2020–2021
China	India	China	China	China
India	China	India	India	India
Japan	**South Korea**	**South Korea**	Saudi Arabia	**South Korea**
South Korea	Japan	Canada	**South Korea**	Canada
Taiwan	Canada	Taiwan	Canada	Saudi Arabia
Canada	Taiwan	Saudi Arabia	Vietnam	Vietnam
Indonesia	Mexico	Japan	Taiwan	Taiwan
Thailand	Turkey	Vietnam	Brazil	Brazil
Turkey	Germany	Mexico	Japan	Mexico
Mexico	Thailand	Turkey	Mexico	Nigeria

Source: IIE, Open Doors Report.

high proportion of its domestic students who study overseas, compounded by a shrinking population of traditional college-aged youth due to the country's low fertility rate. At this critical juncture, universities have adopted internationalization reforms just to stay afloat with enough students. As mentioned earlier, internationalization is defined as the increasing effort by schools to recruit and retain international students. Encouraged through government funding schemes, South Korean universities are adopting internationalization reforms in the hopes that they will attract students from outside South Korea and compete in the global student marketplace. In effect, the South Korean government provides financial assistance to support inbound students but not outbound students.

The South Korean approach to global higher education parallels the South Korean approach to globalization more generally. In South Korea, globalization is best understood not as a force that challenges the power and sovereignty of the nation-state, as defined by the anthropologist Arjun Appadurai, but as a state-managed process through which the South Korean government sets policies in education, science, and technology to remain competitive as a nation-state relative to other nation-states, as argued by the sociologist Gi-Wook Shin.[31] Locally, this is referred to as the segyehwa drive, which was a globalization campaign that began in the 1990s under the Kim Young Sam administration and was a continuation of the country's modernization process. Internationalization reforms in the higher education sector are one facet of the segyehwa drive that aim to raise the global profile of South Korean universities and thereby raise the global profile of South Korea as a nation-state. Internationalization reforms can also attract international students as a way to counteract South Korea's shrinking pool of domestic students. Such an approach to globalization and subsequently internationalization reforms in the higher education sector affect a wide range of higher education activities, from university curricula to microlevel student interactions.[32]

But due to a limited inflow of international students to South Korea, universities have begun to turn to their attention to domestic students who may otherwise study abroad. For example, the Korea Advanced Institute of Science and Technology, one of the premier research universities in South Korea, offers 80 percent of its classes in English, even though South Korean students constitute over 90 percent of its enrollment, effectively offering an English language curriculum for South Korean students within South Korea. Scholarship on international student mobility is opening up the possibility of regarding South Korean students who study abroad not as a distinct population but like any other South Korean students who face an increasingly precarious future overseas and at home.[33] In a 2018 special issue of the *Journal of Intercultural Studies*, Shanthi Robertson, Yi'en Cheng, and Brenda Yeoh highlight how youth can aspire to an overseas education both "on the move" and "in place" as they remake their present realities through the physical act of studying abroad as well as through abstract desires to study abroad.[34] Student immobility, as opposed to mobility, reflects how all students can internalize global aspirations whether they go overseas or not.[35]

It is precisely this globally minded but locally bound population that universities in South Korea seek to capitalize on as they create new educational products to attract more students. The higher education strategist Rahul Choudaha calls this group "glocal" because they are characterized by their desire "to earn the social prestige and career edge offered by foreign education without having to go very far from home."[36] South Korean universities have effectively created new student markets by providing novel learning opportunities at home and drawing in students from within their own borders.[37] And these efforts seem to have palpable results, as the number of students coming from South Korea to US colleges and universities has been steadily shrinking since 2010 (see figure 1.2).

Flexible Universities

The ebb and flow of students across California and South Korea render visible the considerable agency of universities as they flex their

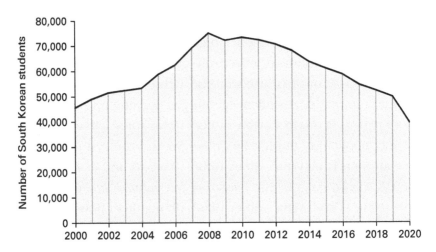

Figure 1.2
South Korean students in US higher education, 2000–2020.
Source: IIE, *Open Doors Report.*

institutional advantages on a global scale and capitalize on students' global aspirations. Indeed, universities are not static in their arrangement nor are they simply embedded within a more expansive economic, political, and societal force called globalization. They are much more flexible in their reach and constitution. They also do not just respond to the mobile trajectories of students. They are themselves exerting agency over this process. Each university constantly shifts it priorities in malleable and profitable ways that collectively pattern student mobility flows across the world.

The flexible university, then, is how we can better understand higher education reform in the context of globalization. Scholars have discussed the strategies that students and their families undertake to pursue higher learning in order to become competitive within the global economy. But these studies primarily focus on the individual while neglecting to examine the institutional arrangements by the universities that these so-called flexible citizens attend. However, a growing number of scholars have begun to prioritize the institution more centrally in our understanding of international student mobility.[38] Immense credit is due to Yasmin Ortiga, whose early theorizations on the flexible university provided the starting point for my thought process on this subject. Ortiga's book *Emigration, Employability and Higher Education in the Philippines*, published in 2018, illustrates how private universities in the Philippines shift resources to produce graduates that meet overseas labor market demands in conjunction with state efforts that prioritize this.[39] Within this arrangement, students are not just customers but also commodities, or as Ilkka Kauppinen, Charles Mathies, and Leasa Weimer describe them, "vessels of economically valuable knowledge," who bring financial resources and increase institutional prestige.[40] In other words, universities create new educational products in order to attract more students, who then become a form of currency for universities to augment their status in the global pecking order of higher education.

In California, under increasingly market-driven conditions, community colleges have positioned themselves as promising transfer gateways into the UC schools for international students who aspire to attend but may not be admitted right away. These community colleges are using their particular institutional advantage to capitalize on the global aspirations of a new stream of students so that they may benefit from increased tuition dollars and global recognition. The end result is that the California higher education system as a whole is repurposing its transfer pathway once designed for domestic students to meet the needs of an additional stream of students. Such a phenomenon shows how a higher education system designed to serve the needs of its local community can unexpectedly become global and flexible. Interestingly, this community college pipeline into the UC schools is frequently used by South Korean students, who seek out this transfer pathway in order to gain admission into the selective universities of California.

Meanwhile in South Korea, universities have created new learning spaces designed to recruit and retain South Korean students who may otherwise study abroad, especially as large numbers study in the United States. These universities have opened special colleges that offer an American liberal arts curriculum, taught entirely in English, by American faculty members recruited from overseas. This instrumentalist approach to internationalization capitalizes on the desires of South Korean youth to attain an American education through targeted institutional objectives. In this case, universities are not just creating new educational products to attract more students; they are creating an entirely new educational experience by systematically "importing" American higher education in order to expand into "glocal" student markets within their own borders. Such an arrangement reveals the incredible range and scope of flexible strategies undertaken by universities to draw in more students and capitalize on their global aspirations. It also reveals the unconventional ways in which South Korean students can now gain entry into selective universities in South Korea.

These novel institutional arrangements across California and South Korea certainly present South Korean students with an array of choices in pursuing higher learning abroad or at home. But the notion of choice is illusory because students become the very commodities that benefit universities. They enroll at universities that offer them the opportunity to do so, and in turn, those universities capitalize on their global aspirations as they themselves desire to be recognized as global institutions of higher learning. This then creates new markers of legitimacy for students, who encounter assumptions of class privilege because their universities tout them as affluent and mobile. Indeed, Sora wanted to ensure that her classmates knew that she wasn't one of "those rich international students" at UC Berkeley. Universities may offer students more choices, but the very creation of those choices shapes the student experience in profound ways.

Furthermore, students do not make choices in a vacuum but instead are influenced by numerous actors, who also capitalize on students' global aspirations. Education agents, admissions recruiters, special purpose high schools, quasi-regulatory bodies, and governmental agencies abound within a larger industry of global higher education. Each individual and institutional actor works in tandem with universities' student recruitment efforts. These "systematically interlinked technologies, institutions, and actors that facilitate and condition mobility" are forms of migration infrastructure.[41] Collectively, they create "spaces of intermediation" within global higher education and act as migration brokers who further shape student mobility flows.[42] Each broker has tangible effects on the choices that students make. Those choices have deep and lasting consequences on students' mobile trajectories.

In this book, I hope to call into question the notion of the unfettered, globetrotting student pursuing higher education all over the world. Students may be presented with an array of choices in their pursuit of higher learning. But those choices are created, mediated, and implemented by a range of different actors operating across the global higher education enterprise that are much more flexible than previously imagined.

Journey of the Book across California, South Korea, and Beyond

This book is the cumulative product of over a decade of studying, researching, and working in higher education in California, South Korea, and Washington, DC. Officially, it is my way of joining three distinct research projects that I undertook while I was living in each of those locales. At the same time, many of my insights "from the field" are also gleaned from personally navigating higher education as a student, staff member, and professor. Having worn these different hats over the last decade, I can better contextualize higher education from each of these vantage points as I engage with the ongoing debates in the field. I also draw from my own experience navigating three distinct ruptures in higher education: the global financial crisis, the election of President Donald Trump, and the COVID-19 pandemic. This book complements its scholarly contributions on international student mobility with my personal accounts of navigating higher education crises to highlight important fissures during a postrecession decade of much anxiety and uncertainty.

I begin this book with the global financial crisis that peaked in 2008 and the deep recession that followed. In the wake of the crisis, I joined UCLA as a doctoral student in the education department between 2009 and 2014, just as the crisis unleashed its full effects on the California higher education system. My own experience as a student was undeniably tied up with the topics I write about, such as vanishing state funds, skyrocketing tuition, student protests, and, of course, the sudden influx of international students on California campuses. Now, with a lot more training and the advantage of hindsight, I can make sense of those experiences with a scholarly eye. They form the beginnings of this book.

During those tumultuous years as a graduate student, I learned how to be a researcher through my dissertation on the internationalization of higher education in South Korea. Just as the Great Recession spurred deep organizational changes across the California higher education system, it did so across higher education systems in places like South Korea, which I was keen to understand as a budding comparativist. From 2011 to 2012, while I was a doctoral student, I joined Yonsei University in Seoul as an international exchange student funded by a Fulbright fellowship to conduct my dissertation fieldwork. The project's earliest questions focused on uncovering implicit assumptions within internationalization reforms through close examination of an international college housed inside Yonsei. I have long finished writing my dissertation, but as any scholar will tell you, one never fully shuts the door on a research project when trying to make sense of something as complex as social phenomena. In this book, I have revisited my dissertation more holistically with an entirely different theoretical lens and methodological approach as I connect what was happening in South Korea to what was happening in California at a time of immense financial instability.

The second rupture was the election of Donald Trump as President of the United States in 2016. At that time, I was a newly minted PhD and had been working at UC Berkeley since 2014, first as a postdoctoral scholar and then an administrative staff member. Seemingly overnight, the campus turned into a hotbed for student activism and a target for far-right demonstrators. My American colleagues wrung their hands over the deleterious "Trump effect" on international student flows to American campuses. What is intriguing about my experience, though, is how little most South Korean students I encountered cared about Trump. As the program director running the day-to-day operations of the Center for Korean Studies, I worked closely with South Korean students and was also conducting a research project on their student experiences. They were more concerned with getting good grades and what they would do after graduation and didn't concern themselves much with open displays of racism or violent clashes between neo-Nazis and Antifa happening regularly on their own campus. When I inquired about these things during interviews, they simply shrugged them off and talked about other reasons why they would or wouldn't study in the United States that had very little to do with American politics and much more to do with their ability to secure a decent job.

It became increasingly clear to me that the Trump effect took hold more strongly among my American colleagues than South Korean students at UC Berkeley. Nonetheless, institutional changes affected the international student experience because, whether those students liked it or not, they were enmeshed within the structural realities of the institution in which they enrolled. It is this more nuanced understanding of the Trump effect that provides an important backdrop, but not the central focus, to the international student experience in this book.

The third rupture was the COVID-19 pandemic. In 2020 higher education activities around the world came to an abrupt halt before transitioning to an unprecedented virtual format. By then, I had been a faculty member at Georgetown University since 2018. I was fortunate in that the greatest disruption that I personally faced was my inability to teach classes in person or use my campus office. My research activities went virtual, too. My original plan was to travel to Seoul to interview education agents, most of whom are part of small recruitment agencies concentrated in the Gangnam area, but I had to cancel my travel plans and conduct all interviews over Zoom. Because of the word-of-mouth nature of this particular industry in South Korea, it was quite difficult to network with agents virtually and establish the rapport necessary to set up interviews. But as the pandemic raged on throughout the completion of this book, I had to make do with what was possible while mostly in lockdown at home.

Meanwhile, the world of global higher education felt as if it were coming apart. Public health conditions disrupted international student mobility at first, but subsequent travel bans and visa cancellations continued to prevent international students from coming to campus, even when domestic students were allowed to return. The rupture caused by the pandemic was not just about the virus itself but also encompassed compounding legislative efforts and growing racism and xenophobia, in the United States and all over the world. During this time, I became involved with a number of DC-based organizations to advocate for the removal of harmful US government restrictions on international students. In the last stages of writing this book, I was also authoring white papers and opinion pieces and giving virtual talks and webinars that championed policies that would facilitate the arrival of international students to the United States. But while advocacy work involves making bold claims and declarative statements, as a scholar, I must admit that the scope and magnitude of this rupture are still uncertain and hence my position on the matter is still unsettled. What is becoming increasingly certain to me, though, is that the scope and magnitude are immense and that the financial constraints and increased competition for students already in place since the Great Recession will only intensify under current conditions.

But, as I said, this book is officially the product of three distinct research projects. The formalities of higher education research require me to outline the technical details of those projects, which are as follows: I conducted participant observations and semistructured interviews across Berkeley and Seoul. I conducted my observations primarily at UC Berkeley and Yonsei University, where I attended numerous student events and sat in on classes when allowed. I also attended international education fairs, conferences, and information sessions in both physical and virtual spaces to observe student recruitment practices. Additionally, I interviewed a total of eighty-three students, faculty members, administrators, and other professionals at UC Berkeley and nearby community colleges; at Yonsei University, including its international college; and across the broader industry of global higher education. Last, I collected documents to contextualize my observations and interviews, including university mission statements, strategic plans, deans' statements, promotional materials, enrollment statistics, institutional reports, faculty CVs, syllabi, news articles, and online message board postings in English and Korean. A more extensive discussion of my research process can be found in the Methodological Appendix.

As a scholar, I have tried to take a reflexive approach by making clear my own social location within my analyses. I have used myself—that is, the multiple identities that I hold as an academic, a woman, a Korean American, a speaker of fluent English and serviceable Korean, among others—as a research tool in eliciting views and reactions. This approach can be antithetical to other, more traditional studies of the university, which often have an interest in measuring the impact of various activities happening on campus but have a tendency not to critically examine the underlying cultures of that institution. Indeed, for scholars housed within, funded by, and otherwise entrenched within the inner workings of universities, taking a critical approach to the very institutions that employ us can make for a deeply uncomfortable study. Nonetheless, my positionality has undoubtedly shaped my scholarship. I share this information because I do not claim objective authority over higher education in California or South Korea, or that I give voice to any of my interviewees, who are perfectly capable of speaking for themselves. The chapters that follow reveal most tellingly my own process of making sense of all that I have observed, analyzed, and contextualized. I present all of this as part of my earnest engagement with the ongoing debates in higher education and its adjacent fields so that, hopefully, the reader finds the end result a meaningful scholarly contribution.

Organization of the Book

I begin by showing how universities create the pathways that allow students to be internationally mobile. Chapter 2 examines UC Berkeley, where a sizable proportion of international students have entered, many of whom come from South Korea. It shows how the California higher education system reconfigured its community college pipeline into a novel admissions pathway that capitalizes on the global aspirations of students from South Korea. It also tells the story of Jessica, a South Korean student enrolled at UC Berkeley in the 2010s when these dramatic reforms unfolded.

Chapter 3 brings us to Yonsei University, widely considered the most global university in South Korea after it opened an international college. It shows how Yonsei reconfigured its international college into a novel admissions pathway that capitalizes on the global aspirations of students from South Korea. It also tells the story of Audrey and Yuri, both South Korean students enrolled at Yonsei in the 2010s during the early years of the international college's operations.

From opposite sides of the world, universities in Berkeley and Seoul have created novel pathways to pursue higher learning abroad and at home for students from South Korea. Chapter 4 focuses on the students who made the choice to enter either UC Berkeley or Yonsei by taking advantage of the universities' flexible arrangements. It connects students from different class backgrounds attending different universities as they are similarly commoditized in their global aspirations. It problematizes the concept of "choice" and challenges assumptions about internationally mobile students.

Expanding on the contradictions of choice, the next chapter turns to the stakeholders that allow students' choices to come to fruition. Chapter 5 maps out the ancillary people and organizations that abound within a larger industry of global higher education. It shows how these individual and institutional actors reinforce the global student supply chain between Berkeley and Seoul as they funnel students to specific universities according to market demands.

Chapter 6 highlights important lessons emerging from the post-recession decade in global higher education. It also provides an updated account of Jessica, Audrey, and Yuri, who have now graduated from UC Berkeley and Yonsei and pursued their professional lives. It then closes with some reflections on the future of international student mobility.

2

A Pathway into UC Berkeley

When I worked at the University of California, Berkeley in the mid-2010s, first as a postdoctoral scholar and then as the program director of the Center for Korean Studies, I was often in close proximity to South Korean students. One such student, Jihun, was enrolled not at UC Berkeley but at a nearby community college located thirty minutes east in Pleasant Hill. Jihun's goal was to transfer to UC Berkeley and become a film major after finishing two years of coursework at the community college. He had not been a strong student while attending high school in South Korea, he told me, and his low grades disqualified him from the competitive tracks to get into a selective university there. His mother urged him to consider college in the United States, where he might find more possibilities for academic success. As a late bloomer with newfound focus and drive, Jihun aimed to do well in his community college classes, after which he could then transition into the next stage of his collegiate ambitions at UC Berkeley.

Over time, I began to notice other South Korean students like Jihun and the diverse pathways that they took to arrive at UC Berkeley, especially as community college transfers. Historically, the California higher education system was set up to provide a continuum of educational opportunity from community colleges all the way up to major research universities for California residents through the 1960 California Master Plan for Higher Education. But as the system faces continuing budget cuts in the aftermath of the Great Recession and beyond, California higher education institutions have sought out more international students who pay higher tuition fees in order to generate more revenue. And many of these international students first enter community colleges before transferring to the UC schools. This pathway, originally designed for California residents, has been repurposed to meet the needs of an additional stream of students, a significant proportion of whom come from South Korea.

So how do universities create the very pathways that allow students to be internationally mobile? In this chapter, I show how one university in Berkeley did so by repurposing its transfer pathway from the community colleges to capitalize on the global aspirations of South Korean students. Adopting a structural approach, I begin by analyzing the California higher education system under the economic and political conditions of the postrecession years, when the system faced many challenges. I examine how budget cuts and legislative changes led to dramatic changes in California's colleges and universities, especially a rapidly growing proportion of international students across the UC campuses. Yet these changes have not gone uncontested: since 2017 the massive influx of hopeful applicants resulted in strict admissions quotas across the UC schools for international students, in part as a result of public outcry over their increased presence. Nonetheless, the California higher education system as a whole collectively continued to facilitate entryways for international students through its robust transfer system.

As UC Berkeley responded to domestic pressure by restricting access to international students, this enabled neighboring community colleges to recruit international students more aggressively as they positioned themselves as accessible transfer gateways. But South Korean students who entered UC Berkeley through the community college pipeline encountered hostility as simultaneous transfer students at UC Berkeley and international students in California. I share the story of Jessica, a South Korean student studying at UC Berkeley in the 2010s, as the university contended with financial pressures and domestic pushback. Her experience reflects the lived realities of the students who became entangled within the California higher education system's contradictory efforts to expand into global student markets.

Designing a Higher Education System for the Masses

In the fall of 2021 UC Berkeley offered admission to 4,889 transfer students, and 95 percent of these offers went to transfer students from California community colleges.[1] The total undergraduate population in the same semester was approximately 31,000, so these transfer students constitute a small but vital portion of the student body. The ability to transfer from a community college into a prestigious research university highlights the best of the California higher education system. The system was in large part designed by one man, Clark Kerr, the primary architect of the 1960 California Master Plan for Higher Education. A professor of economics who later moved into administration, Kerr organized the state's public higher education institutions into a coordinated system of research universities, state universities, and community colleges. In a series of lectures delivered in 1963 and published as *The Uses of the University* later that same year, Kerr outlined what he called "the inevitability of concentration," wherein a handful of universities would be best equipped to undertake federally funded research, train graduate students, and offer doctoral degrees; the so-called middle institutions would be devoted to undergraduate teaching; and the remaining majority of institutions would prepare the bulk of California's population for employment through skills-based training.[2]

Kerr designed the system in part to meet the challenge of educating a generation of baby boomers, but his Master Plan continues to have consequences for all students in California more than half a century later.

Kerr's tripartite system coordinated what was previously a disparate collection of competing colleges and universities into a single system that could produce superior research, attract distinguished faculty members, educate the best and brightest students, and still provide broad access to high-quality tertiary education for California's growing population. According to the Master Plan, the top eighth of graduating high school seniors would be guaranteed a place at the University of California; the top one-third would enter California State University (Cal State); and anyone with the capacity to benefit from instruction could enroll in the state's two-year community colleges.[3] Community college graduates who maintain certain grade point average thresholds would also be guaranteed placement into a UC or Cal State university. Kerr set UC Berkeley as the crown jewel of this tripartite system after having served as the university's first chancellor from 1952 to 1957. But his overarching framework made it possible for any talented student in California to move through a continuum of educational opportunity and graduate from a place like UC Berkeley regardless of where one started.

California's higher education framework has been equally celebrated and criticized. The celebration is well deserved: the Master Plan was able to deliver high-quality, low-cost tertiary education to an unprecedentedly large population and did not limit access on the basis of race or gender. This ethic of inclusion was remarkable at a time when many elite universities in the United States admitted only White men. Since its foundation, the California system has served an incredible number of students: by 2017 college enrollment in California increased tenfold, to 1.9 million students enrolled full time, while the state's population had not even tripled.[4] All three systems—the UC, Cal State, and California Community Colleges systems—have grown tremendously with the addition of new campuses to accommodate the exploding demand for higher education. Today, the UC system is the largest research university system, the Cal State system is the largest four-year university system, and the California Community Colleges system is the largest higher education system in the United States.

The Master Plan also allowed each type of institution to concentrate its resources in particular areas, while the system as a whole met broad societal demand for higher education through a robust transfer system. The system was designed to have the majority of California students begin at a community college and receive a general education through two years of coursework. That coursework would then be recognized by any UC or Cal State university as credit toward a bachelor's degree, as a significant proportion of those students transferred to a four-year university. The historian John Aubrey Douglass notes, "No other public or private university in the nation included such a high percentage of transfer students . . . [which] made California's higher education system unique, both in the high dependence on access through the junior college and in the number of students who then matriculated to a public four-year institution."[5]

The Master Plan's influence radiates beyond California to higher education systems in other states and even other countries. The higher education scholar Simon Marginson argues that its approach to access and growth, particularly through open access and demand-led participation, has become the norm in most higher education systems across the world. On a global level, what we refer to as "Americanization" in comparative higher education discourse could more aptly be described as "Californization."[6] An example Marginson gives is China, where since the late 1990s a growing proportion of its tremendous population has aspired to leave behind poverty and agricultural work and enter the middle class. Parallel to what happened in California in the 1950s and 1960s, China's leaders and policymakers are now faced with the prospect of meeting the explosion of demand for higher education and have looked to California's example for inspiration. Scholars at UC Berkeley have seized on this trend, especially at the Center for Studies in Higher Education, which regularly hosts summits and workshops for delegations from China for exactly this reason.[7]

But criticism of the Master Plan abounds, particularly around the core tension of expanding access while also increasing selectivity. John Aubrey Douglass further explains how the Master Plan caused the UC and Cal State universities to increase selectivity while pushing burgeoning demand for higher education toward the community colleges in ways that correlated with students' socioeconomic backgrounds.[8] It is in fact extremely difficult for a low-income student to get into UC Berkeley. Educationists criticize the "tracking" of students as laborers or professionals because it reproduces social stratification based on the needs of a capitalist labor market, often in racialized ways.[9] And while the UC system initially rejected the use of the SAT in its admissions criteria, in 1968 it began to require SAT scores from applicants, leading to even tighter admissions standards. The incorporation of the SAT as a metric, which has been widely criticized for implicit bias, was seen as a way not to improve the admissions process but to limit access to the UCs. This practice also likely contributed to the sorting of students along the lines of class and race in California.[10]

Today, the UC schools use a holistic admissions approach across thirteen variables, which include grades, rigor of courses, special talents or achievements, and academic performance relative to the educational opportunities available in a student's high school. In 2020, in part as a response to the COVID-19 pandemic, the UC and Cal State systems suspended the use of standardized test scores in the admissions process before fully eliminating their use as of 2021.[11] Even so, as California higher education institutions reach full capacity and turn down many highly qualified students, admissions standards at places like UC Berkeley have become fiercely competitive. In fact, following the elimination of test scores, the university received a record 112,800 applications for its 2021 intake, followed by another record 128,100 applications for its 2022 intake.[12] Such astounding numbers reflect the fiercely competitive nature of UC Berkeley's admissions process and the impressive qualifications of its student body.

Jessica: A Model Student at UC Berkeley

I first met Jessica through my work at the Center of Korean Studies. Born and raised in Seoul, Jessica told me that her college friends call her by her adopted American name rather than her given Korean name. When we met at the beginning of the 2017 fall semester, Jessica was entering her senior year at UC Berkeley and stepping into her newly elected role as the president of one of the largest Korean student clubs on campus. We connected when the Center and Jessica's club cosponsored an event to bring a well-known politician from South Korea to speak at the campus, and Jessica was the lead organizer for that event. What struck me about Jessica was her high level of competency in how she went about all her activities. She exemplified what one might consider a model student: intelligent, hardworking, and ambitious. After working with her on the event, I invited her to meet with me again so that we could chat about her student experience.

Jessica is exactly the kind of high-achieving student that UC Berkeley seeks to attract as it increases its selectivity. She could have attended any number of universities. During the application process, she also applied to UCLA, Michigan, Brown, Cornell, NYU, and Emory and received several other offers. Her choice illustrates how well UC Berkeley attracts competitive students from outside California. In fact, having Jessica study in California was a dream of her father's. He knew that his tenacious daughter would thrive in the United States, unlike her less adventurous younger brother, who just wanted to stay in South Korea. Jessica's father wanted her to gain the worldly perspective that comes from studying abroad. The San Francisco Bay Area, with its diverse cultures and dynamic Silicon Valley, offered an ideal place for Jessica to do so.

Upon entering UC Berkeley, Jessica became a political economy major with a concentration in the political economy of China. She became interested in this subject because of her father's import-export business that he operated between South Korea and China, she told me. She hoped to join his company someday, an ambition that her father encouraged. When Jessica was a young girl, she sometimes tagged along on her father's business trips to Shanghai, Hangzhou, and Suzhou. So she selected political economy as her major, even though she found the course prerequisites challenging. Jessica nonetheless persisted through them.

> Political economy major in Berkeley is somehow very competitive. What I mean by competitive is it's hard for international students, for Korean students, because we have certain classes that we have to meet the minimum requirements. All my friends . . . they couldn't meet the requirements, so they had to change their major to global studies. That really scared me . . . So I did all the readings, everything. I just did everything that the syllabus asked me to do, not even Spark Notes, just reading. Like Mesopotamians, Gilgamesh, old readings I cannot even understand in Korean. I asked my mom to just buy those books written in Korean and send to me in Berkeley. I did everything that I can do. Otherwise, I cannot understand. I couldn't give up . . . At the end, I got a good grade. I was in the top third.

Even before college, Jessica was no stranger to hard work and intensive studying. As a child, she had a team of private tutors and extramural classes to help her succeed academically. Compared to her friends, she enjoyed learning English and excelled in English conversation, which helped her develop into a confident and outgoing college student. She was able to hone her language skills through the specialized coursework at her high school, where students were expected to practice conversation with a native speaker from the

United States. The very fact that her private high school, Ewha Girls' High School in Seoul, even offered such courses hints at the exclusive educational tracks open to Jessica. Indeed, the influx of students like Jessica begs a larger question of how accessible institutions like UC Berkeley really are for the majority of students, especially as budget cuts to the UC system have further decreased admission rates.

Budget Cuts and Angry Students

The year 2009 was a watershed for the California higher education system. In the aftermath of the Great Recession, the UC system lost over $813 million in funding from the California state government. The UC Board of Regents immediately voted to increase student fees by a breathtaking 32 percent that same year. While smaller fee hikes assessed annually had preceded the recession, the higher fee hikes led to large-scale student demonstrations across the UC campuses. Students across the Berkeley, Davis, Los Angeles, Riverside, and Santa Cruz campuses occupied buildings, shut down campus operations, and issued lists of demands to campus administration in response to the dramatic fee hikes.

The year 2009 was also when I began my studies in the California higher education system as a doctoral student in the education department at UCLA. My first year was accompanied by alarming fee hikes assessed mid-year and equally alarming fee hikes assessed each year thereafter until I graduated, and beyond. Though the fee hikes affected undergraduate students the most, they also threatened graduate student funding, which subsidized student fees in exchange for work as research and teaching assistants. These positions quickly dried up when the funds required to offer them increased suddenly, and positions that were promised to graduate students as part of funding packages were suddenly gone. This early period of my studies was also marked by student walkouts from classes, sit-ins within campus buildings, and regular disruptions to daily campus life—some of which I participated in with my classmates as we advocated to restore the integrity of public higher education and for our own well-being.

Across the UC campuses, the demonstrations took on the flavor and rhetoric of the concurrent Occupy Wall Street movement by framing the fee hikes as academic capitalism run amok and hapless students as the 99 percent. A slogan of "Occupy Everything" sprang up on signs and in graffiti on campus buildings. At UC Berkeley, students allied with Occupy demonstrators to form a gathering of over a thousand people, who called themselves "Occupy Cal" and set up an encampment in the middle of Sproul Plaza. And similar to how city officials responded to Occupy Wall Street in Manhattan, campus authorities also used excessive force trying to contain student demonstrations by deploying campus police armed with batons and riot gear. The most distressing of these incidents took place in 2011, when student demonstrators, who identified themselves as Occupy UC Davis, set up an encampment on the campus quad. As peaceful demonstrators sat motionless on the ground with bowed heads, police officers used pepper spray at point-blank range directly into students' faces. The incident was caught by onlookers with cell phone cameras and immediately went viral, sparking outrage that eventually led to the resignation of then UC Davis Chancellor Linda Katehi.

While student fee hikes continued, the intense spectacle of student demonstrations brought national attention to the issue of dwindling financial support for public higher education in California. The left-wing magazine *Dissent* published a critical piece describing the situation in California as a sign of the end of public higher education in the United States. The authors, Aaron Bady and Mike Konczal, write,

> It's important to remember this chapter in California history because it may, in retrospect, have signaled the beginning of the end of public higher education in the United States as we'd known it. It's true that when the Great Recession began in 2008, state budgets crumbled

under a crippling new fiscal reality and tuition and debt levels began to skyrocket. It was also in the context of the California student movement that the slogan "Occupy Everything, Demand Nothing" first emerged, in 2009, when students occupied campus buildings in protest against budget cuts, tuition hikes, and staff cutbacks, and were crushed by the same kind of overwhelming police force that was later mobilized against Occupy encampments across the country.[13]

But in 2009 the California higher education system was no stranger to budget cuts, which began decades earlier with legislation in the late 1970s. At that time, the US economy was experiencing sudden inflation as a result of rising oil prices and stagnant incomes. California homeowners were especially worried about soaring home values that would result in property taxes that outpaced earnings. In 1978 California voters passed Proposition 13, a ballot measure that capped property tax rates to 1 percent of property values and no more than 2 percent annual increases thereafter. By effectively freezing property taxes to a miniscule percentage of home market value, Proposition 13 created a permanent tax break for homeowners in California. It also had consequences for education since it reduced local property taxes, which had previously been the greatest funding source for local school districts. Meanwhile, the California Supreme Court mandated in several key decisions during the 1970s that differences in wealth between local school communities were inequitable and that local school funding would be redistributed by the state. The California government was now responsible for local school funding, but with insufficient funds. It began to shift its budget allocation from universities to local schools and community colleges. And as the state weighed other priorities, both university and K–14 funding have accounted for an increasingly smaller share of its budget allocation since the late 1970s. The cuts have been most strongly felt in the UC system, where state funding per full-time student decreased from $23,000 in FY 1976–1977 to $8,000 in FY 2016–2017.[14]

Despite this longer-term trend, the more dramatic student fee hikes and subsequent student demonstrations beginning in 2009 are still a pivotal inflection point in the history of California higher education because they brought to the fore of national consciousness large-scale state disinvestment in public higher education. Seemingly overnight, the American public became much more aware of rising tuition costs and developed a vested interest in the role of higher education as a public good. Indeed, the UC student demonstrations of the late aughts in part laid the groundwork for today's national discourse on free college and student loan forgiveness. Public higher education in California has become a flash point within this discourse.

Racialized Admissions

When I first arrived as a doctoral student at UCLA in 2009, I was initially surprised at how seamlessly I could blend in on campus. As an Asian American woman, then in my twenties, I found myself suddenly part of the demographic majority on my campus, something I had not experienced before as a person of color who attended college in the Midwest and a master's program on the East Coast. That fall, 40 percent of incoming freshman students at UCLA identified as Asian American, the largest demographic on campus. To be clear, this proportion did not include international students from Asia, who at that time constituted a much smaller proportion—though that was soon to change.

In 1960 Clark Kerr's Master Plan made no mention of racial or ethnic representation, but these issues have since been hotly debated in the California higher education system. In the 1960s and 1970s, many universities adopted a quota system for minority students: for instance, by setting aside 16 slots out of 100 in an incoming class, as in the UC Davis School of Medicine. In 1978 the Supreme Court ruled that a racial quota system was unconstitutional but that race could be used as "one factor among many" in the admissions process, ushering in an era of affirmative action in college admissions. However, with the passage of Proposition 209 in 1996, California became the first state to prohibit state government institutions from considering race and ethnicity (as well as sex) in public employment, contracting, and education. This decision effectively ended affirmative action in the California higher education system. It also negatively impacted Black, Latinx, and Indigenous students, who were disproportionately "pushed out" of UC campuses.[15] The adverse effects of Proposition 209 on underrepresented minorities that extend well beyond college admissions continue to be a key point of contention in the debates on affirmative action.

At the heart of these debates lies the ambiguous position of Asian American students in the college admissions process. After Proposition 209 took effect, the enrollment rate of Asian American students increased across the more selective UC campuses. Conservative groups have seized upon this statistical trend as evidence that Asian Americans benefit from race-blind admissions, even though experts deny any causal relationship.[16] Conservative groups also argue that colleges and universities impose a higher bar for Asian Americans than other applicants when using race-conscious admissions and have even paraded Asian Americans themselves as "racial mascots" in their legal battles.[17] In short, Asian Americans are no longer considered an underrepresented minority within undergraduate admissions and are often pitted against other students of color in attempts to dismantle affirmative action.

The stereotype of Asian Americans as high achievers—and the implication that other minorities should just try harder—resonates within these conservative efforts. Pundits often ascribe Asian American academic achievement to inherent cultural values. But in their book *The Asian American Achievement Paradox*, published in 2015, the sociologists Jennifer Lee and Min Zhou show how a confluence of factors, including restrictive immigration laws, close-knit ethnic communities, and the effects of positive stereotyping held by teachers and guidance counselors, all contribute to the high academic performance of Asian American students.[18] Nonetheless, the most lasting effect of the tiger mom stereotype is a widely held belief that Asian American achievement is the result of a special dynamism or discipline among Asians. This belief feeds into the idea that Asian Americans are perpetual foreigners unable or unwilling to assimilate into the American cultural mainstream.

The image of the perpetual foreigner corresponds to another, more pernicious stereotype that reflects generalized anxiety around the growing presence of Asian Americans across UC campuses. As Asian American students have become the majority demographic across many UC campuses, some students refer to those schools with pejorative acronyms, for example, by calling UCLA the University of Caucasians Lost among Asians. This acronym portrays Asian Americans as foreign invaders whose presence threatens a shrinking White student body. The story of former UCLA student Alexandra Wallace best demonstrates White anxiety around the increased presence of Asian Americans on UC campuses. In 2011 Wallace, a White student, posted a YouTube video of herself making anti-Asian racist remarks that went viral. Her chants of "ching chong ling long" and complaints of the "hordes" of Asian students—a term Wallace presumably intended to conflate both American students with Asian heritage and international students from Asia—who refuse to follow "American manners" reflect how Asian Americans are seen as incompatible aliens who threaten the cultural integrity of UC campuses. Notably, Wallace was never disciplined for the video, though she eventually withdrew from UCLA.

Meanwhile, international student enrollment has increased substantially across the UC campuses as a result of budget cuts. Historically, the undergraduate student body at most UC campuses almost exclusively came from California, with international students typically never reaching more than single-digit proportions.[19] Parallel with the student fee hikes, however, UC campuses have begun to admit more undergraduate students from outside California while assessing significant student fees to make up for declining state budgets. This is consistent with research that reveals a strong negative relationship between state appropriations and nonresident freshman enrollment at public research universities.[20] Much of the nonresident enrollment increases in California have come from international students, the majority from Asian countries, with the proportion of international students among undergraduate students jumping significantly across many UC campuses. While I was studying at UCLA, for example, international students accounted for only 3 percent of incoming freshman students when I arrived in 2009, but that proportion jumped to 18 percent by 2012.[21]

While anti-Asian racism predated the influx of international students from Asia across the UC campuses, it has certainly sharpened in the last decade. Charges of threatened campus cultures proliferated among students, faculty, and administrators as the proportion of international students increased. Here I recall my own experience teaching in the UCLA Writing Programs from 2012 to 2014. I joined the Writing Programs as an instructor for undergraduate academic writing courses while finishing my dissertation. These courses were offered to all students who needed academic writing instruction. But as an instructor, I was often warned of the rampant plagiarism and cheating among international students—a term my White colleagues used as a carefully cloaked reference to Asian students—who were viewed as not understanding the norms of academic integrity in American higher education. Additionally, UCLA mandated a minicourse to prevent plagiarism for international students specifically, rather than all students generally. While this "management" of international students may not constitute outright racism, it does constitute what the higher education scholars Jenny Lee and Charles Rice characterize as "neo-racism," an institutionalized form

of cultural superiority enacted over students deemed culturally inferior.[22] This was exactly what I encountered studying and working at
UCLA as an Asian American woman, during a time when there was
a sudden influx of international students from Asia, at a campus
where the large presence of Asian American students was already
in contention. I found myself navigating thinly veiled nativist attitudes not just confined to conservative discourses but quite preva-
lent among my liberal colleagues.

Hence, anti-Asian racism previously directed at Asian American
students has expanded to encompass international students from
Asia across the UC campuses. Nowhere has this rancor metastasized
faster than within college admissions, where Asian students are now
positioned in a zero-sum admissions competition with domestic students from California. Admission into the UC system was always a
contentious process; this time, international students from Asia are
under fire, fueled by undertones of racism and xenophobia. Perhaps
most tellingly, the UC regents approved for the first time a policy
that capped the proportion of nonresident undergraduate student
enrollment at 18 percent across five UC campuses and at existing
levels at the Berkeley, Irvine, Los Angeles, and San Diego campuses,
beginning with the 2017–2018 academic year. Paradoxically, the UC
system has reinstituted a strict quota system, this time for nonresident students, just as the proportion of international students from
Asia increased—justifying this policy under the rationale of "putting California students first."[23]

Jessica: Becoming Californian

Though Jessica was initially surprised by the large presence of Asian
and Asian American students on her campus, she flourished in such
a diverse setting. She had an image of America as "full of White people," and her original dream of American higher education included

ivy-covered brick buildings, autumnal foliage, and preppy students tossing a frisbee on the quad, a vision drawn from media portrayals of liberal arts colleges on the East Coast. But when she arrived in California, she found herself surrounded by what she jokingly noted as "black-haired people who speak English." Despite the initial culture shock, Jessica embraced American campus life, California style. She consciously chose to get involved in diverse extracurricular activities, including a student club focused on leadership development for Korean students. She also chose to live in the UC Berkeley dormitories her first year there so that she could make friends.

Part of the reason that Jessica was able to adjust so easily to her new environment is that she enrolled in the intensive English program at UC Berkeley Extension before beginning college. There, she took classes to improve her English and learn about American culture while meeting students from all over the world who were there to do the same. In addition to courses on language and culture, the program instructed students on practical matters, such as how to set up a local bank account and where to find furniture and basic amenities. California colleges and universities are incorporating more transition programs such as these to ease international students' adjustment to American campus life. At UC Berkeley, such programs are open to undergraduate and graduate students, as well as to visiting and precollegiate students such as Jessica.

Over time, Jessica grew accustomed to the norms and expectations of California, so much so that she found it difficult to reenter life in South Korea. Because her daily life in California was in English, she found that she needed some time to readjust to Korean whenever she visited home during summer and winter breaks. She also forgot Korean words or phrases so frequently that her friends in South Korea commented on her clunky diction. When Jessica returned to Seoul the summer after her junior year to undertake a competitive internship at the South Korean National Assembly, she found the work environment intense and suffocating. She described how her outspokenness, a trait highly valued at UC Berkeley, became a liability for her within a professional setting in South Korea.

> It wasn't clear for me what they asked me to do. If I try to [ask for clarification], it sounds very offensive to them, I guess, or very unnecessary to them . . . The National Assembly internship was also an unpaid internship. So I feel like I have to speak up more. I know there was such a high demand to work there, but it doesn't mean that they have a right to exploit my labor. It doesn't mean I can be a slave. That's what I thought . . . Somehow since I came here and studied more and I'm in the most liberal part of the US, I just couldn't accept it . . . I have a right to say something or speak something when it doesn't make sense. But my parents said, "Hey, take it easy, it's part of the culture."

Jessica is a trailblazer who may no longer fit in so easily in South Korea. She came to the United States by herself at the age of eighteen and thrived amid the diverse cultures she encountered in California. As she neared the end of her college career, she contemplated her next steps. She was reaching out to her friends who worked in the tech industry, relationships she developed through the Korean student club, where she was president. She was also exploring the possibility of continuing her studies in an MBA program in the United States. She considered returning to South Korea, but that possibility just did not excite her at this stage.

> I'm not sure what I'm going to do in Korea because I don't want to just work in Korea. The reason why I don't really want to go back to Korea is because I'm not here just to get a diploma from Berkeley. It's a good certification. But as I said, I studied hard, I learned a lot, and I experienced a lot. As I major in something and I learned something, I have to utilize it in the future. Why do I just study and throw it away and just go back to my life five years, ten years before, to where I just came from? Because my father sent me here to be more global, to experience more. Why do I have to go back to that narrow society and fit myself to that society? So that doesn't make sense to me. If I didn't enjoy my life here . . . definitely I'll go back. But so far, I'm

pretty satisfied with my life in general. Although Berkeley is tough, I like this competitive atmosphere.

One factor that gave her pause, however, was that she missed her family. When she shared as much to her parents, she was taken aback by their response. As she anticipated, her father encouraged her to be brave and find her own path. But her mother, who was previously reluctant to send her only daughter overseas, told Jessica that she was happy to see her thrive in California and encouraged her to stay. Jessica was relieved but also a little sad. Nonetheless, as she did with most things in her life, she took things in stride: "I'm realistic, but it doesn't mean I'm pessimistic. I'm very ambitious and resilient."

When the Master Plan Meets a New Reality

When he finalized the Master Plan in 1960, Clark Kerr could not have guessed that the California higher education system would experience the influx of international students that it has today. More international students study in California than in any other state. Likewise, California colleges and universities have expanded their student pools beyond domestic students, and UC Berkeley is no exception. But what may be surprising to know is that, for well over a decade, international students have constituted a larger proportion of community college transfers than freshman students at the university (see figure 2.1).

While budget cuts have hit the UC system the hardest, community colleges have also suffered substantial losses relative to past economic downturns in California. Between 2007 and 2012, community colleges faced cuts totaling $1.5 billion.[24] The California legislature increased system-wide student fees substantially, with the largest fee hike assessed at a 28 percent increase for the 2012–2013 academic year. But the additional revenue from student fees

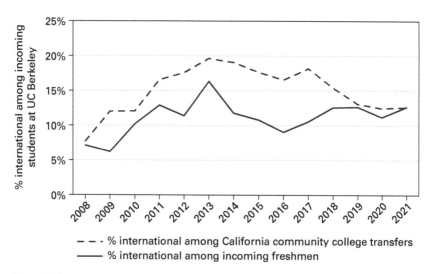

Figure 2.1
Proportion of international students among incoming students at UC Berkeley, 2008–2021.
Source: UCOP, "Fall Enrollment at a Glance."

has been insufficient in making up for the loss of state funding, leading to even lower state funding per full-time student than was already in place.

Community colleges have responded to the budget cuts in a variety of ways. The majority have reduced the number of course sections or dropped courses entirely, reducing their overall course offerings for both credit-bearing programs and noncredit continuing education areas. The number of faculty and staff employed at community colleges has also decreased, and salary and benefit freezes have been implemented. Meanwhile, class sizes have swelled and workload hours have increased for both faculty and student service staff. The cumulative result of these changes has resulted in a restriction of access across community colleges that were intended to be open access institutions. Between 2008 and 2012, participation rates in community colleges by adults in California decreased by 21 percent.[25]

But bucking this trend is international student enrollment, which has actually increased in the last decade. In fact, California leads the way in international student enrollment in community colleges, with fifteen of the top forty community colleges with the highest international student enrollment across the United States.[26] While governed by a central body that determines student fees, these campuses can individually assess at their own discretion additional fees to international and other nonresident students. At Santa Monica College, for example, the community college with the largest international student enrollment in the state, California residents pay $46 per credit hour while international students pay $307, an amount nearly seven times the resident fee, which does not even account for the mandatory health insurance fees that only international students pay.[27]

Nonetheless, the international student rate at community colleges such as Santa Monica is much cheaper than the tuition at UC schools, which is one of the biggest draws for attending a community college. Students are able to pay significantly lower fees for two years of coursework that can then be recognized as transfer credit at a UC school. Many community colleges tout their relatively cheaper tuition and successful transfer rates into the UC institutions as a recruitment tool for international students. Some have even developed a reputation as feeder schools into specific campuses. De Anza College and Diablo Valley College, for example, are both well known for their high transfer rates into UC Berkeley. And international students have constituted a third—and in some years nearly half—of the total number of students who transfer from De Anza and Diablo Valley to UC Berkeley each year for the last decade.[28]

Community colleges like De Anza and Diablo Valley also offer bridge programs that target international students. These programs allow international students admission to the college while foregoing English testing requirements such as the TOEFL, provided that they instead enroll in precollege English language coursework, available for an extra fee. They also offer student services catered to the needs of international students, such as visa and housing assistance, as well as social activities and cultural excursions.

Additional study programs, also available for an extra fee, provide professional study aides who hold workshops and study sessions that teach international students how to succeed at an American campus. Between the years 2010 and 2014, when the immediate effects of the budget cuts unfolded across California community colleges, revenue-generating programs for international students grew substantially while cost-generating extracurricular activities, including international student clubs and international celebrations, decreased dramatically.[29]

These examples speak to how, in response to dwindling revenue from state sources, California community colleges are customizing special programs for international students able and willing to pay for them. A major part of their marketing strategy is to highlight their accessibility as a selling point and position themselves as promising transfer gateways into UC schools. Indeed, community colleges have become attractive options to international students exactly because UC schools are tightening admission rates and restricting access for international students. The cumulative effect across the California higher education system is the institutionalization of an unexpected international student pipeline into UC Berkeley, as community colleges position themselves as accessible pathways.

A Contentious Learning Space for South Korean Students

UC Berkeley is under siege! At least it is according to a provocative Facebook post published to the Facebook page of a student club in 2015 that railed against those who entered as community college transfers. The student who authored the post believed that the university's prestige was diminishing in South Korea because of the intrusion of a large number of South Korean transfer students who, this student believed, were of inferior academic ability. Though the post was eventually deleted, a screenshot was published in an article in *Berkeley Opinion*, a student-run publication by and for the Korean student community. The author of the article, another student, attempted to dismiss the polemical claims made in the post as the particular views of a single person.[30] But numerous commentators left harsh remarks to both the original post and the follow-up article that further criticized South Korean transfer students. The incident created a kerfuffle on campus and reignited the label of "freshman students" for those who entered in their freshman year, to distinguish them from "transfer students" who transferred from community colleges.[31] Increasingly, South Korean students used these labels to describe themselves and others within their community.

It is important to note how community colleges are an integral part of the Korean student experience at UC Berkeley. While South Korean students have constituted the third-largest group of international students across US colleges and universities for the past two decades, they were the largest group of international students to enroll in community colleges in the United States between 2007 and 2012.[32] Those years correspond almost exactly with the same years during which the proportion of international students among community college transfers to UC Berkeley grew considerably. Moreover, South Korean students were the largest group of international students at the university between 2006 and 2011—surpassing even students from China and India during that time—which also corresponds with the marked increase of international students among community college transfers to UC Berkeley. In short, the community college transfer pipeline as an increasingly popular pathway into UC Berkeley is strongly connected to South Korean students in particular.[33]

Historically, South Korean students who pursued higher education overseas in the 1990s and 2000s were thought of as trying to escape the competitive education system in South Korea. Compared to other groups of US-bound international students, students from South Korea were mostly interested in the personal and experiential aspects of studying in the United States.[34] These students were believed to be academically less competitive but nonetheless financially advantaged enough to study abroad. They were also considered to be highly desirable in the job market when returning to South Korea upon graduation. Their global cultural capital, signaled by the prestige of a US university degree and their English fluency, gave them competitive advantages over their peers who did not study abroad. Such advantages fostered resentment toward outwardly mobile students, who were seen as undeserving of their advantages that were acquired by money rather than aptitude. Yet these perceptions have largely disappeared in the last decade, as more South Korean students have studied abroad, a larger proportion of whom have come from highly competitive high schools in South Korea. Accordingly, the competitive advantages of studying abroad have also disappeared in the last decade, as the South Korean job market has flooded with overseas degree holders. And in the aftermath of the Great Recession, youth in South Korea face such high rates of unemployment that even those who have graduated from selective universities in the United States are anxious about their future prospects.

It is under these conditions of economic precarity that South Korean students at UC Berkeley have transposed a prior class stigma around study abroad onto the institutional particularities of the California higher education system in order to find new competitive advantages. Specifically, the discourse of "freshman students" versus "transfer students" is how some South Korean students were able to distinguish themselves from other South Korean students on their campus. Freshman students pointed to transfer students' novel way of entering to position them as inherently different. They accused transfer students of being interlopers who entered through a side door that bypassed the more rigorous way in which freshman students supposedly entered. They also frequently referred to transfer students as "those rich international students" able to leverage their financial means to study abroad, by simply paying extra fees and entering the California higher education system without having to prepare for the SAT or TOEFL, or even maintaining good grades in high school. In short, South Korean students have reinterpreted their narrowing access to UC Berkeley versus their expanded access to community colleges to signify their ability to succeed versus their ability to pay.

South Korean students have also transposed the same racialized discourse used against international students generally onto transfer students specifically. Freshman students frequently pointed to transfer students' poor linguistic ability in English and propensity to plagiarize and cheat—racially coded portrayals of international students that they themselves encountered at UC Berkeley—as evidence of transfer students' inferiority. These students wielded the language of racialization against members of their own community in the hopes that doing so would shift racialized tropes onto someone else.[35] And similar to how racialized discourses often operate between "us" versus "them," the discourse of "freshman students" versus "transfer students" then enabled freshman students to point to an obvious scapegoat when their UC Berkeley degree no longer guaranteed them success in an uncertain job market back home.

Indeed, a contentious learning space has emerged for South Korean students at UC Berkeley that is deeply entangled with the UC system's ambiguous reception of international students. Ironically, restrictions on international student enrollment in the UC system have enabled neighboring community colleges to recruit more international students by positioning themselves as accessible transfer gateways. The broader tensions around international student enrollment in the UC system then created localized tensions for South Korean students, who constitute a significant proportion of community college transfers at UC Berkeley. These students must negotiate dual stigmas around international students and transfer students simultaneously. This contentious learning space for South Korean students has only become more pronounced as the

UC regents continue to squabble over the appropriate proportion of international students. More broadly, these tensions underscore how profoundly institutional priorities can shape not just students' international mobility but their daily experiences on campus.

Jessica: Finding Legitimacy

Jessica told me during our follow-up chat that she is actually a community college transfer at UC Berkeley. This was not something that she hid from others, but it also was not a fact that she shared right away with her peers or throughout her professional networks. She first enrolled in 2013 at De Anza College, a community college located an hour south of Berkeley in Cupertino, before transferring in her junior year. When Jessica was applying to colleges as a high school student in Seoul, she and her family consulted with an education agent, who recommended this route as an ideal pathway for her particular situation. According to the agent, attending a community college would allow Jessica to study in the United States without having to prepare for the SAT or TOEFL, something that Jessica lost energy for after having studied so intensely for the national college entrance exam in South Korea. Of the many community colleges that she could have attended across the United States, Jessica's parents prioritized schools in California because they wanted their daughter to be geographically closer to them in South Korea. They especially liked the safe environment of Cupertino. But most important, De Anza boasts of a high transfer rate to UC Berkeley, where Jessica wanted to study.

Since beginning her studies at De Anza, Jessica was intent on transferring. She started her studies in the intensive English program at UC Berkeley Extension for a semester and got a taste for Berkeley life before moving to Cupertino. While studying at De Anza, she completed her general education requirements by carefully selecting courses that aligned with UC Berkeley's breadth requirements. She also enrolled in more difficult courses that she thought would make her a competitive transfer applicant, unlike the South Korean students she met at De Anza who opted to take the easier ones. Knowing that the many South Korean students who attend De Anza are not all able to transfer to UC Berkeley, she explained how she avoided making friends who might affect her ability to do so.

> For about two, three years I didn't join any Korean clubs in De Anza, not at all. So even though they know me, that I'm Korean, they asked me to just show up, I just didn't go. There's a lot of rumors, a lot of stuff just going around. It's not like I was screening, but this college is not a good place to make ideal friends for me because everyone can get into college . . . I don't really feel like it was necessary to hang out with them. So I just had a few friends who really studied hard, same goals, transferred to good schools. Less than three people.

Although she isolated herself socially, Jessica excelled in her studies. She had a 3.98 grade point average by the time she completed her coursework at the community college. She printed out the *U.S. News & World Report* top thirty university rankings and taped them to her bedroom wall when it came time to apply to four-year universities. She was admitted to UC Berkeley as well as a handful of other selective schools, which made her parents proud. They were especially happy to see her enroll at one of the most renowned universities in California and begin her coursework in political economy. And when Jessica finally arrived, she allowed herself to become more involved with the Korean student community. She joined a Korean student club that focuses on developing professional networks, and after a year she was elected the club's president. She used her new leadership position and the contacts she made at her summer internship at the South Korean National Assembly to invite a high-profile political figure from South Korea to come speak at UC Berkeley.

Is Jessica one of "those rich international students"? Perhaps. But any notion that she is academically inferior to her peers disappears in the face of her scholastic and extracurricular record. In fact, she treated her community college peers as inferior, not "ideal friends" for a woman who aspired to attend UC Berkeley. Ultimately, Jessica's hard work, meticulous planning, and determination enabled her to gain admission to an excellent university. Still, the fact that she limited her social activities at De Anza and omits her time there on her professional profile underscores how conscious she is of how her background as a community college transfer appears to her peers. Jessica has internalized the discourse around "transfer students" and treated the fact as something to obscure. Many other community college transfers from South Korea whom I met at UC Berkeley used the same strategy of omission in their professional presentation. Jessica even actively avoided other South Korean students at De Anza, knowing that many of them may aspire to transfer, but not all can succeed. Admissions has become a zero-sum competition even among South Koreans. Only after arriving at UC Berkeley did Jessica integrate with the Korean student community to eventually become one of the community's most visible leaders, a position that made her even more careful about disclosing her particular way of arriving.

Summary

Higher education reforms across the California higher education system illustrate how postrecession domestic realities intersect with South Korean students' global aspirations. While the system was originally designed to serve California's rapidly growing population in the 1960s, in the aftermath of the Great Recession a half century later, the system has sought out more international students to make up for state budget cuts. However, the influx of international students across the UC campuses was met with domestic pushback, in no small part due to the forces of racism and xenophobia. Hence, admissions became bifurcated, with California community colleges seeking out international students more aggressively and UC campuses restricting their enrollment. Meanwhile, international students who sought admission to the UC campuses often did so by first attending community colleges and then transferring, leading to the repurposing of the transfer pipeline to capitalize on South Korean students' global aspirations. As a result, South Korean students at UC Berkeley have created artificial distinctions between who belongs and who does not related to the diverse pathways they took to arrive. This new discourse reflects their anxiety around their contested status as simultaneous transfer students at UC Berkeley and international students in California.

Jessica's story demonstrates how one bright, motivated student from South Korea navigated an unusual pathway into the California higher education system and negotiated admission into UC Berkeley. Jessica, a high-achieving student and one of the most visible leaders of the Korean student community, downplayed her own background as a community college transfer. She was acutely aware of how her particular pathway into the university positioned her vis-à-vis her classmates from South Korea, who were wont to label her with descriptions that delegitimize her intelligence and ability. Indeed, the California higher education system's contradictory efforts to recruit international students can shape students' experiences in very real ways.

3

A Pathway into Yonsei University

On a humid August morning in 2011, I entered the auditorium of Baekyang Hall to attend the international student orientation at Yonsei University. Everyone excitedly chatted with each other in a mixture of English and Korean until a noticeably blond man walked onto the stage. Surprised at seeing a non-Korean working at this South Korean university, everyone quieted down and listened with rapt attention. Speaking in English with a distinct American accent, he introduced himself as the Associate Dean of International Affairs and a faculty member at Yonsei. He shared a story of how, just like us, he had first arrived at Yonsei as an international student, an experience that led to his long-term professional trajectory in South Korea.

This chapter takes us halfway around the world to a university in South Korea that is widely considered to be the country's most global institution of higher learning. But to understand Yonsei's ambitions, we must contextualize its development in relation to American higher education. Indeed, the American man who led the international student orientation at Yonsei was one of the founding faculty members of Underwood International College (UIC), which bills itself as an American-style liberal arts college housed inside Yonsei. I would spend the next year immersing myself in this curious amalgamation of American and South Korean higher education models as part of my doctoral dissertation research.[1]

South Korean universities have undertaken institutional reforms to align themselves with the standards of excellence that prevail in the United States. These standards draw on the American liberal arts model as the hallmark of the college experience. Yonsei opened UIC in 2006 and created an American-style liberal arts college that would attract international students from all over the world. Since then, many South Korean universities have opened similar colleges. But while these colleges have come to symbolize the higher education sector's international student recruitment efforts, most students who enroll are, in fact, South Korean citizens. Due to a limited inflow of degree-seeking international students to South Korea, these colleges have turned their sights to domestic students to make up for enrollment deficiencies among international students.

So how do universities create the very pathways that allow students to be internationally mobile? In this chapter, I show how one university in Seoul did so by repurposing its admissions pathway into an American-style liberal arts college to capitalize on the global aspirations of South Korean students. Adopting a structural approach, I begin by analyzing how the American liberal arts model has become a commercial enterprise across Asia, as universities integrate American standards of excellence to compete with universities in the United States. In South Korea, universities have launched American-style liberal arts colleges as distinct learning spaces intended to attract international students, especially in response to a rapidly shrinking pool of domestic students. But the hoped-for wave of international students never arrived. As a result, these colleges have reconfigured their admissions standards and categories to recruit globally minded South Korean students.

With the establishment of UIC, Yonsei positioned itself as the premier global university in the country. But the special role that the college plays has also transformed the student experience in a paradoxical way: UIC sells the American college experience to a mostly South Korean student body. I reveal how profoundly institutional reforms have shaped the student experience for Audrey and Yuri, two South Korean students studying at Yonsei in the 2010s during the early years of UIC's operations. Their experiences reflect the lived realities of the students who became entangled within Yonsei's contradictory efforts to expand into global student markets.

Reimagining the American Liberal Arts Model in Asia

A 2015 article entitled "The Slow Death of the University" appeared in *The Chronicle of Higher Education* and lamented the "death" of the university via the demise of humanistic inquiry.[2] According to the author, the literary theorist Terry Eagleton, universities are facing a gradual decline because manager-like professors and tuition-hungry departments are pursuing entrepreneurial strategies at the expense of the humanities. The article opens with a vignette of Eagleton taking a tour of a university in South Korea, led by the university's president, only to gawk at how the school did not offer any humanities courses. Eagleton's point was that the degradation of the humanities that was happening across universities in the United States and Britain was also happening across universities all over the world, even in far-flung places like South Korea.

Humanistic inquiry was canonized as part of the American college experience in the Yale Report of 1828. The Yale Report reaffirmed a classical curriculum rooted in Ancient Greek understandings of an education deemed to be essential for human development and civic life, and that was distinct from a vocational education. Today, humanistic inquiry is a core part of an American liberal arts education, which emphasizes two years of interdisciplinary learning across a broad range of subjects in the arts and sciences followed by two years of study in a single subject area. The Association of

American Colleges and Universities defines a liberal education as a "philosophy of education that empowers individuals with broad knowledge and transferable skills, and a strong sense of values, ethics, and civic engagement."[3] This particular learning model also encourages critical thinking, writing ability, information literacy, and a high level of student-teacher interaction.

Since the Great Recession, however, scholars have lamented the erosion of liberal arts education across institutions of higher learning in the United States. For example, Richard Arum and Josipa Roksa point out that an undergraduate curriculum founded upon critical thinking, complex reasoning, and writing is on the decline because undergraduate learning has become underprioritized under conditions of economic austerity.[4] Along the same lines, Derek Bok points out that today's college students are not attaining the skills that should be cultivated through a liberal arts education because professors are more concerned with the administration of their departments rather than the art of teaching.[5] Taking a Marxist position, Christopher Newfield criticizes how the public university's mission of broad cultural and human development that distinguished it from a capitalist society has been replaced by the simpler goal of increasing revenue, leading to the degradation of humanities instruction within public colleges and universities, where most American students enroll.[6] Stanley Aronowitz further argues that students themselves choose to study in fields that promise economic payoffs rather than liberal transformation, especially as all but a handful of universities have become credential mills that merely teach students to adjust to existing social arrangements.[7] In short, these scholars believe that the decline of liberal arts education is a byproduct of the capitalist restructuring of higher education.

But what is happening across Asia actually challenges the assumption that a liberal arts education is inevitably the victim to academic capitalism. As many Asian universities also enter the global student marketplace, university leaders have been forced to pay attention to institutional quality. In particular, they have turned to universities in highly developed countries in the West to define excellence in teaching and learning, especially as those institutions dominate across global rankings. One striking result of cross-border quality assurance practices is the proliferation of colleges and universities throughout Asia that adopt the American liberal arts model: seminar-style classrooms, student-centered pedagogy, instruction in English, residential living, and an intellectual grounding in humanistic inquiry.[8]

An early rendering of this kind of learning institution, Ritsumeikan Asia Pacific University, opened in Japan in 2000. The institution's mission statement emphasizes collaborative debate-type learning, group work, discussion, communication skills, and intercultural understanding. Courses are held in both English and Japanese, and students are required to be able to communicate in both languages by graduation. Another example is the Asian University for Women, which opened in Bangladesh in 2008. It seeks to expand access to higher education for women of the local region while billing itself as a liberal arts college that emulates the Seven Sisters in the United States. Additionally, the proliferation of international partnerships between American and Asian universities—such as the ones between Yale University and the National University of Singapore that formed Yale-NUS College in Singapore in 2011, New York University and East China Normal University that formed NYU Shanghai in China in 2012, and Duke University and Wuhan University that formed Duke Kunshan University in China in 2013—have further enabled students to obtain an American liberal arts education without having to physically go to the United States. The geographer Yi'en Cheng notes that these institutions combine international exposure, citizenship education, and an explicit or implicit American liberal arts model to produce graduates who are active participants in a global economy.[9]

It would be easy to lodge a critique of American hegemony against this arrangement, and certainly scholars have condemned the "Anglo-Saxon paradigms" after which Asian universities have been modeled.[10] But it is important to remember that these arrangements are created and implemented by various decision-makers within Asia. In the book *Transnational Education Crossing "Asia" and "the West,"* published in 2017, the education scholar Phan Le Ha notes how Asian university leaders themselves have adopted a deficit model as they implement reforms that transplant American learning models into Asian institutions.[11] Phan's critique draws from the cultural critic Kuan-Hsing Chen's 2010 book *Asia as Method*, which describes an imaginary West that functions as an opposing entity to learn from or catch up with.[12] Both Phan and Chen posit a dialectical relationship between Asia and the West that ascribes significant agency to autochthonous actors within Asia. Indeed, the underlying motivation behind the establishment of these new learning institutions is not to adopt the American liberal arts model simply for its own sake, but rather to offer an educational product that meets international standards and prepares students for the opportunities and challenges of globalization. In other words, the goal of these new learning institutions is to become purveyors of global knowledge within a global student marketplace.

How ironic it is, then, that scholars lament the demise of liberal arts education in the United States as an unfortunate consequence of academic capitalism. When we examine what is happening in Asia, we actually see the proliferation of liberal arts education not despite but exactly because of academic capitalism. Notably, a liberal arts education has become commercially appropriated into a marketable product in the capitalist restructuring of higher education across Asia.[13] By offering a liberal arts education, Asian universities are simultaneously conforming to American standards of excellence while profiting from them. And perhaps nowhere has the need for greater student markets been as dire as it is in South Korea, where the American liberal arts model has been looked to as an antidote to challenging financial conditions.

South Korean Higher Education in Crisis

When pundits predict the future of American higher education, they often point to the looming demographic shifts in the United States that will reduce the traditional student pools of eighteen- to twenty-four-year-olds from which colleges and universities can recruit.[14] For the United States, this scenario may take place in the not-too-distant future, as the fertility rate dropped below the population replacement level and continued to decline after the Great Recession. For countries in East Asia, especially South Korea, it is already a reality. South Korea has had a falling fertility rate for many decades already. Following the baby boom during the years immediately after the Korean War, the fertility rate declined dramatically. It dropped below the population replacement level by the 1980s, and since 2018, dropped to less than one birth per woman and continued to decline since.[15]

As the national fertility rate continues to fall, the national education attainment rate is skyrocketing. Before the Korean War, most South Koreans did not even complete primary school. Today, South Korean youth are the most educated in the world, with 70 percent of twenty-five- to thirty-four-year-olds attaining higher education.[16] By comparison, in the United States, the rate is 52 percent.[17] But as education attainment levels have risen, so, too, have education costs. The country's high-pressure culture around education created a predatory shadow education market, consisting of cram schools and private tutors, which often adds significant costs that private households must finance.[18] Indeed, South Koreans spend significantly more on private education expenditures than do households in most other countries across all levels of education. This high cost of education is often blamed for the country's staggeringly low fertility rate, as potential parents weigh the future costs of educating their children.

In addition to the shrinking number of college-aged youth, South Korea stands out for the large number of students who study abroad.

South Korea, with a higher education student population of 3.3 million, sends over 101,000 degree-seeking students overseas each year; many more South Korean students go overseas for language study or temporary exchange programs.[19] Again, for comparison, the United States, with a higher education student population of 20 million, sends just over 84,000 degree-seeking students overseas each year.[20]

Starting in the 2000s, higher education institutions in South Korea began to see decreasing numbers of new incoming domestic students. In the year 2000, there were almost 820,000 new incoming domestic students across the higher education sector, but in 2020, there were just under 625,000 students—a reduction of 23 percent within two decades (see figure 3.1).[21] Schools in provincial areas outside of the Seoul metropolitan region face an even more acute student shortage, and many have closed or merged due to financial pressures.

As a response to the domestic student shortage, the South Korean government introduced a series of policies in the 2000s and 2010s intended to internationalize the country's higher education sector as a means to attract more students from overseas. The most direct initiative to do so is the Study Korea Project, which actively

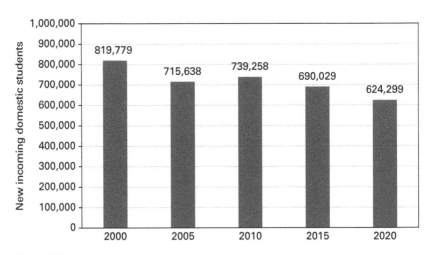

Figure 3.1
New incoming domestic students in South Korean higher education, 2000–2020.
Source: KEDI, *Brief Statistics on Korean Education.*

targets international student enrollment through scholarships and publicity programs. Other initiatives sought to improve the standing of South Korean universities in global rankings by improving their research capacity. For instance, the Brain Korea 21 Project poured money into a small group of universities to encourage faculty members to produce more articles in indexed journals. And as global rankings began to account for the proportion of international faculty members, the government launched the World Class University Project, which invited overseas scholars to South Korean universities through special subsidy programs. Subsequent initiatives, such as the Brain Korea 21 Plus Project, have continued to augment the research capacity of South Korean universities in more qualitative ways, such as enhancing graduate education.

These policies underscore the growing sense that universities in South Korea need to improve institutional quality to attract more international students, a need that has become critical as an economic response to a serious domestic student shortage.[22] They also highlight the considerable role of the state in creating the conditions for universities to draw in international students, especially in a centralized higher education sector such as South Korea's. Indeed, as a direct result of these policies, universities have adopted aggressive reforms that have spurred deep organizational changes, including a culture of research productivity, the adoption of English as the academic lingua franca, the recruitment of overseas faculty members, and an increasingly centralized form of institutional governance. One particular reform encapsulates those changes all at once: the emergence of international colleges.

Establishing an International College in South Korea

Yonsei University opened Underwood International College (UIC) in 2006 as a pioneering development in the South Korean higher education sector: an international college housed inside a South

Korean university that adopts an American liberal arts curriculum, taught entirely in English, by American faculty members recruited from overseas. The college takes its name after Horace Grant Underwood, the American Presbyterian missionary who established Chosun Christian College (renamed Yonhi College), the first modern college in Korea established in 1915 that would eventually become Yonsei University. In the spirit of its namesake, UIC aims to bring the outside world to South Korea. The college's conceptual design is based on the notion of "inbound globalization," a term frequently used by the former university president, Jeong Changyeong (also spelled Jung Chang Young), to imply that international students and scholars are an important component of achieving world-class status. Inbound globalization is also meant to counteract "outbound globalization," whereby South Korean students go overseas in large numbers. The founding dean, Jongryn Mo, proclaimed that by "establishing UIC, Yonsei University is affirming its belief in inbound globalization that international students and international faculty members must be brought into Yonsei University to create a global campus. With a global campus, a world-class education will follow."[23]

As globalization has become a focal point of higher education, university leaders increasingly refer to their global mission while seeking out international students and scholars as a way to attain global recognition.[24] In fact, the very rhetoric of a global education is what distinguishes UIC from the South Korean university in which it is housed. UIC promises "international knowledge" and "international networks" while claiming to train students to be "international leaders" ready for "international competition."[25] These promises of excellence reflect a trend in higher education reform in which institutions seek to improve institutional quality that is measured by global rankings.[26] By also calling itself an American-style liberal arts college, UIC intentionally conflates the American liberal arts model with its generically global orientation.

This Americanizing agenda is reflected above all in UIC's signature liberal arts curriculum. At UIC, students spend two years studying a common curriculum of humanistic subjects, such as Western and Eastern civilizations, literature, history, and philosophy, within a separate college taught entirely in English. Then students declare a major and take more specialized courses for two years in an established department at Yonsei, taught in either English or Korean. This is in stark contrast to the typical South Korean university student, who immediately specializes in a single subject area and completes four years of study within one department. Soon after Yonsei launched UIC, other selective universities opened similar colleges: Ewha Womans University opened Scranton College in 2007; Korea University opened the School of Interdisciplinary Studies in 2009; and Seoul National University opened the College of Liberal Studies in 2009.

But Yonsei took on the project of Americanization one step further by hiring American faculty members recruited from overseas. In fact, the UIC faculty members are critical to the college's global mission. UIC explicitly articulates a requirement of non–South Korean citizenship in its faculty position advertisements.[27] In practice, UIC recruits faculty applicants who are citizens of a Western country with a PhD from a university in a Western country (in most cases, the United States); this has certainly been the case for all the full-time faculty members hired to teach within the college's signature liberal arts curriculum. At UIC, the knowledge workers themselves—American faculty members recruited from overseas—are brought into a South Korean university setting as a way to deliver on the college's global promise.[28]

What is most striking about UIC is the way it has strategically deployed a particular vision of Americanization as a commercial enterprise. By offering an American liberal arts curriculum, taught entirely in English, by American faculty members recruited from overseas, Yonsei has fully embraced American standards of excellence while cashing in on them. In fact, UIC tuition is double that of most other parts of the university (at approximately 15,000,000 won per year, or $12,000).[29] Yonsei has commercially packaged the American college experience in the form of UIC in order to attract international students to its novel learning environment—and attracting international students was indeed a driving motivation behind the college's establishment. In my conversations with one of the founders of the college, I was told that by establishing UIC and drawing in international students, Yonsei would be able to enroll students outside of the strict quota of domestic students the university is allowed to enroll as set by the Ministry of Education.[30] Seen in this way, Yonsei has created an American-style liberal arts college as a profitable way to align itself with American domination across global student markets and bypass governmental restrictions.

Reconfiguring the International Student

When I was traveling around Seoul interviewing people during my Fulbright-sponsored research year at Yonsei, the South Koreans whom I met sometimes noticed the American lilt in my Korean and asked me at what age I left South Korea. I would then correct them and say that my parents left South Korea in the 1970s and that I'm actually a Korean American born and raised entirely in the United States. Once I shared this information, describing myself as a gyopo in Korean, my interlocutors would express surprise and comment on my impressive Korean language skills. They had mistaken me for a transnational Korean who returned to South Korea after having lived abroad, rather than a diasporic Korean descended from South Korean immigrants in the United States.

South Koreans have codified the differences between the transnational Korean versus the diasporic Korean through media representations of their linguistic ability.[31] Transnational Koreans are portrayed as members of the cosmopolitan elite who moved over-seas for education or work, as signaled by multilingual competency and worldly tastes. They have gained valuable forms of global cultural capital from their overseas experience. Diasporic Koreans are portrayed as unsophisticated Korean Americans, as signaled by their laughably bad Korean. Descendants of immigrants in the United States, they have lost a vital connection to their ethnic homeland or remain "stuck" in a past fixture of South Korea that no longer exists. Such assumptions of linguistic gain or loss also rely heavily on class signaling, as many South Korean immigrants came to the United States without much social or economic capital. Indeed, I was mistaken for a transnational Korean who returned from abroad only when I introduced myself in connection with Yonsei and the prestigious Fulbright program. By contrast, when I was going about my daily encounters anonymously at the market or a coffee shop, South Koreans frequently chastised me for my American accent and awkward Korean phrasing, which signaled to them that I was a low-class Korean American who "forgot" her heritage language.

But transnational Koreans are distinct from diasporic Koreans not only in perceptions of linguistic ability but also because of their return to South Korea, which is how they participate in global circulations and leverage their overseas experience to become members of the cosmopolitan elite rather than immigrants.[32] This is exactly the kind of student whom I frequently met studying at UIC. In fact, many UIC students whom I encountered were not international students at all but South Korean citizens who had returned to South Korea after an extended period of living abroad. One such transnational returnee was Audrey. Audrey was born in South Korea and grew up in Turkey, where her father's job in the South Korean diplomatic corps brought the whole family. She attended international schools throughout Europe before graduating from an international high school in Germany, where the instruction was in English. When I asked her why she had come to UIC, she told me that she did not consider herself to be what she called "a typical Korean" and therefore wanted to pursue an American liberal arts education. She also wanted to reacquaint herself with her country of citizenship, especially as her parents planned to return to South Korea eventually. So when she turned her sights to South Korea as an alternative to the United States when applying to college, she discovered UIC and enrolled there.

While the college may want to admit as many international students as possible, it actually has trouble doing so. Consider the possibility from the student's perspective: Why UIC? Why would one travel thousands of miles away from one's home country to enroll at an American-style liberal arts college in South Korea? The international students who do come, often from China and Vietnam, are induced by scholarship money, I was told. Meanwhile, the college has looked to transnational Koreans currently living abroad, such as Audrey, as a way to make up for international student enrollment deficiencies.[33] It has even created a new admissions category called Overseas Korean, which underscores the college's formal recognition of this group.[34]

This new category illustrates the complex reach of the college's recruitment strategy, which is to prioritize students deemed "international" in the admissions process. This new category also circumvents the strict quota of domestic students the university is allowed to enroll since South Korean citizens who complete their K–12 education overseas are also exempt.[35] Indeed, a UIC senior administrator told me that the college had a higher admission rate for Overseas Koreans than domestic students because it could accept such students outside of the quota system. UIC has effectively recognized time spent overseas as an admissions preference and created a special admissions pathway into Yonsei for transnational returnees.

Students are also reconfiguring what it means to be "international" when they pursue cross-border higher education through repatriation. Like Audrey, many transnational returnees whom I met told me that their decision to come to UIC reflected their desire to reacquaint themselves with their country of citizenship within a campus environment that could accommodate their cosmopolitan background. As students who spent years enrolled in overseas schools learning in English, they felt more comfortable with the college's all-English instruction. For these students, who often could not function at a high academic level other than in English, the college served as an English language gateway into a South Korean university.

Audrey, too, felt more comfortable in English-medium classes, even though she was conversationally fluent in Korean. As a political science major, she spoke fondly of the enriching experience of taking liberal arts classes within the UIC common curriculum.

> Overall, the thing I always recommend about UIC to other people who are considering UIC is its liberal arts program. I tell them that we have a really strong common curriculum. We have a really strong liberal arts program. The professors are really good, strong, know their area. That's really unique for Korea, to have that kind of thing. The best thing about my whole experience was to be able to take these diverse classes and have built it up to my major, to see how history and philosophy can also be applicable to international relations and political science, be able to make those connections.

She also found that the college's pedagogical approach allowed her and her UIC peers to excel across their other classes at Yonsei.

> Sometimes, [non-UIC] students and [UIC] students take English courses together. They overlap. There might be fifty of us in the room, but you'll probably notice that it's UIC students who are participating the most. Maybe that's because we're more comfortable in English. Or maybe that's because we're . . . not afraid to ask questions or reply. Most Korean students are very quiet because I think they're more used to lecture-based whereas we're more used to discussion-based classes.

But such a classroom dynamic fostered resentment from her classmates outside of the college. When I asked her to elaborate on the reasons, she added,

People view us as we have this privilege, like we have this advantage
of English because most, well some of us, for me, for my upbringing
and because of my parents. So they view that as being stuck up, or
it's just a natural privilege that I didn't necessarily earn. But it was
very natural for me to grow up and learn English whereas for them
it's not natural.

Audrey's advantages in the classroom certainly indicate deeper
advantages related to her overseas experience and family background. At the time we met in 2012, she had recently graduated
from Yonsei as a political science major and was planning to go to
Egypt to study Arabic so that she could further advance her understanding of the Middle East and pursue a career in humanitarian
work. She described how her unique upbringing inspired her to
pursue interesting opportunities that didn't conform to the expectations followed by most other South Korean students:

For me, I think just growing up abroad and experiencing different
cultures doesn't make you biased towards anyone. When I tell people
that I'm going to the Middle East to study the language, a lot of people
don't understand why I'm doing that when other people are getting
good jobs and everything. But for me, I think the background gives
me more freedom. I don't necessarily consider Korea my home, but
that doesn't mean I consider another country per se my home. I'm
not bound to one country, and I'm not bound to one language.
It gives me the freedom to be able to communicate with people
anywhere. I don't really see myself as having particular boundaries
that tie me down anywhere. Just being able to have different
friends that have all different kind of backgrounds, I think it gives
you a greater understanding of people. So I can basically just do
whatever it is I want to do. I don't have that fear of language. I don't
have that fear of a different culture.

Her worldly ambitions certainly inspired awe and envy among other
students. As a transnational returnee, Audrey was able to leverage
the "rules" of citizenship to "turn displacement into advantageous
placement" against the backdrop of family networks that make it
possible.[36] Her UIC education was integral to how she translated her

diverse educational background into valuable forms of cultural capital and positioned herself as cosmopolitan elite within South Korea.

Reconfiguring the Domestic Student

When I was meeting with UIC students, I made regular trips to Yonsei International Campus, which is adjacent to Incheon Global Campus, an education hub that houses a number of international branch campuses, including SUNY Korea and George Mason University Korea. The hub is located in Songdo, a government-planned city quite removed from South Korea's cultural mecca of Seoul. Without traffic, it takes around ninety minutes to get from Yonsei's main campus to the Songdo campus via direct shuttle bus, and even longer via public transportation. Although Songdo is home to many international campuses, Seoulites joke that the only international feature of Songdo is its location near Incheon International Airport. For UIC, Songdo is significant because that is where students are required to live and study in a residential college environment.

I expected to hear more English spoken at this international campus, but instead I only heard Korean. Strolling around the campus casually observing the students, I could not tell who was enrolled at UIC and who was not. Everyone I encountered wore identical Yonsei hoodies and jackets and spoke in Korean. On occasion, though, I'd hear an English phrase or sentence uttered in the course of an otherwise Korean conversation—which, I would later learn, is the signature way that UIC students speak to each other. These ambiguous distinctions were not just a product of my unfamiliar eye but actually reflected the student body. While many UIC students were transnational returnees, many others were not. Many were South Koreans who graduated from high schools in South Korea. Some students had some early study abroad experience, but they did not live abroad long enough to be classified as Overseas Koreans. In fact, the more students whom I met and interviewed, the more unclear it became what actually distinguished UIC students.

One student whom I encountered was Yuri. The eldest child of "typical Korean parents," as she described, Yuri was born and raised in Seoul. She had traveled abroad for short durations with her family but never lived anywhere else. She attended Daewon Foreign Language High School, one of the premier foreign language high schools in Seoul renowned for cultivating foreign language skills in its students. Yuri attended the school mainly because it could help her gain admission into a selective university in South Korea. Yuri had never considered going abroad for college. She learned English and Chinese through her high school's rigorous curriculum, which made her a competitive applicant when it came time to apply to colleges in South Korea. Upon graduating, she became a student at UIC. When I asked Yuri why she chose to enroll at UIC, she said,

> For me, I was originally preparing for going to normal universities that are taught in Korean. But in my senior year in high school, I got to know about this program, UIC program, at Yonsei. First of all, like Yonsei University, it has a good reputation . . . I hear that there's a separate college devoted to English language instruction. So that was fascinating for me, and that's how I decided to come here. Major courses are interesting, too, but in my freshman or sophomore years, they have this common curriculum program. It's mandatory for us to take history and literature, and that was really fascinating for me. That was also the reason why I applied for UIC, that they kind of bragged about having a strong liberal arts program, at least for the first two years of university. And that's not really common for other Korean universities.

Other UIC students whom I met were similar to Yuri in this respect. They were not transnational returnees but had lived most or all of their life in South Korea. Some had early study abroad experience and some did not. Nearly everyone whom I met graduated from a foreign language high school in South Korea. The most striking similarity they shared was that they had all wanted to attend a university in South Korea and ended up at UIC. Some had applied to other universities in South Korea, or even to a traditional department at Yonsei. A few had been preparing to study abroad in the United States by taking the SAT and Advanced Placement exams during high school but ultimately felt emotionally unprepared to leave South Korea. Moving to a foreign country by themselves at the tender age of eighteen took more than just academic preparation, and these students did not feel ready to go. Because they had not been preparing for the national college entrance exam, they applied to UIC as a de facto option because it was one of the few colleges in South Korea that would consider them on the basis of their SAT and Advanced Placement exam scores. Another UIC student whom I met, who described herself as "good at English," told me that she only applied to programs in South Korea that prioritized English language skills in their admissions process as a strategic way to get into a selective university in South Korea; she did not even consider studying abroad.

While the UIC rhetoric professes that inbound globalization is a way to attract international students to South Korea, the admissions categories and qualifications suggest that inbound globalization is better understood as a pathway back to South Korea for transnational returnees like Audrey. But from the testimony of Yuri and many others, domestic students also end up enrolling in UIC as a way to leverage their existing global cultural capital to enter Yonsei. Just as the college has established an unexpected admissions pathway into Yonsei for transnational returnees, it has also established an unexpected admissions pathway into Yonsei for domestic students who seek entry by capitalizing on their English fluency.

But once these students enter UIC, they undergo a palpable transformation by spending their formative years in an international college. When Yuri first arrived, she was initially intimidated by the large presence of transnational returnees she encountered:

> I was very dormant in my social life at UIC, actually. But that's
> also because I felt left out from the beginning because I just grew
> up here all my life. Like all of my international experience was just

traveling for a bit. I stayed in Toronto in Canada for five months when
I was young. So that was all I had. But all the other students had
international experience for their whole life. That was something
very different for me. And they had different mentalities as well. So I
found it very difficult to interact with them at first. Now it's okay, but
at first, it felt very different for me. So I didn't really participate in a
lot of activities.

Over time, however, Yuri integrated better into the college's academic and social fabric. She became more curious about world affairs
and declared political science as her major. Though she never intended
to go abroad when she entered college, she did so for her junior year.
She spent a year at the University of Zurich in Switzerland as an
exchange student. While living overseas, she met friends from all over
the world and developed a romantic relationship with a Swiss boyfriend. She described how her UIC education and exposure to transnational returnees with diverse life experiences prepared her well for
the unfamiliar people and situations she encountered while abroad:

> I was more or less familiar with speaking or writing in English before
> I entered college. But it really helped me, the four years of training in
> academic English. That's probably why I felt like it was very difficult
> to adjust to college life in my freshman or sophomore years because,
> yes, I read newspapers in English, I watched TV shows in English,
> but it's something different if your schooling is in English. It's a
> totally new experience. I didn't really know that before I entered
> college. But after four years, I'm very much familiarized. I felt the
> power of English instruction during my exchange year. I found
> everything very easy to adjust to because the language was no
> problem for me. If I was a regular Yonsei student who is not as good
> at English as I was, then of course I could go through everything as
> I did. But I think it would've been still more difficult. Also, having
> friends who already have international experiences, that also helped
> me because I got to know what it's like. So I think I became more
> broad-minded in that way, through my friends.

And Yuri is not alone in this transformation. A number of UIC students whom I met shared similar sentiments while highlighting how

their UIC education was fundamental to cultivating a more global outlook.

UIC has, in effect, reconfigured Yuri and others like her from domestic students into global citizens without them having to leave their home country. They could have studied in a traditional department at a South Korean university, but because of their English fluency, they instead ended up at an international college. Once there, they were immersed in an American learning environment surrounded by students who are also South Korean citizens but who come from all over the world. The pedagogical, linguistic, and social life of an international college left a profound mark on their attitudes and worldview. Indeed, as Yuri was completing her last year of college in 2012, she expressed a desire to return to Europe after graduating. Once unimaginable, living abroad was now something that appealed to Yuri. Her UIC education was integral to this transformation.

A Contentious Learning Space for UIC Students

For a week in May, the Yonsei campus is covered in blue flags and tents. Jubilant music blares across loudspeakers. Thousands of students flock to campus donning blue t-shirts to take part in the Akaraka festival, a celebration of school spirit over its rival, Korea University. The school tradition centers around a series of sporting events between the two universities and also features pep rallies, school bands, performance groups, and a K-pop concert (the lineup included "Gangnam Style" singer Psy when I was there). The festival is also where students cement the friendships that will eventually become their professional networks. To facilitate this informal networking, the university designates specific seating areas at the sporting events, where students of each department can sit together to build camaraderie and show their pride as a department. But noticeably absent is an area for UIC students—UIC is not recognized by the university as a formal department—leaving UIC students to fend for themselves during the festivities.

The event organizers likely overlooked these subtle social dynamics for students of the international college. Because UIC projects an image as a distinctly international space intended for international students, the students who attend are assumed to be uninterested in the intimate social networking spaces designed for domestic students. But, as we have seen, the students of UIC are predominantly South Korean. In many ways, the distinction between UIC students and other Yonsei students is a forced structural separation of the college's design. But the college's particular arrangement creates a perception of foreignness around the students who attend despite the fact that most UIC students are South Korean citizens.

Perceptions of foreignness are what distinguished UIC students to other Yonsei students. Other Yonsei students described UIC students as inherently different from the majority student body. They pointed to UIC students' overseas experience and English fluency to mark them as "foreign," even though they acknowledged UIC students' South Korean citizenship. Their descriptions also positioned UIC students in opposition to themselves, which they coded as "normal" or "native." As one Yonsei student told me,

> They don't know the normal Korean norms, and that's what
> makes them impolite at times. They don't know the basic Korean
> etiquettes and Korean manners. [Koreans] think when people speak
> in English, their voice becomes a bit higher, their intonations
> become higher. Sometimes the volume becomes a bit bigger. Koreans
> will think that that's because they want to show off their English.

Interestingly, these comments were shared with me, a Korean American who was interviewing students in English. I began each interview clearly identifying myself as a Korean American and an international exchange student at Yonsei, which positioned me as an outsider. It was my outsider status that allowed such strong descriptions of UIC students to flow freely among other Yonsei students. Their excoriation of

UIC students, whom they imagined as affluent, mobile, and foreign, excluded Korean Americans such as myself. Yonsei students felt safe relaying their criticisms of UIC students to me, presumably because I was an outsider who was not competing with or challenging their position within a hierarchy of students.

Indeed, Yonsei students' binary of who is "foreign" and who is not was entangled with the institutional arrangements of their university rather than a literal critique of citizenship status that can target a Korean American like myself. It was a similar dynamic to how "freshman students" distinguished themselves from "transfer students" at UC Berkeley, which I discussed in chapter 2. Yonsei students adopted the language of racialization to find differences among UIC students that conflated the way in which UIC students entered the university with their foreignness. The prevailing attitude among Yonsei students was that UIC students were able to gain admission to the university through a separate admissions system that capitalized on their overseas experience and English fluency as a side door into one of the most elite universities in South Korea. As one Yonsei student told me, "I've heard that some normal Korean students think that UIC students . . . just came to Yonsei University just because of their language skills, not in other qualities"—other qualities meaning hard work and merit.

Perceptions of foreignness were only enhanced by the curricular requirements of UIC. Those who study in UIC's liberal arts curriculum are required to split their time between the college and an established department, where they take more specialized courses to fulfill the requirements of their major. But each of those departments have formal admissions processes for the majority of students, who apply to and enter those departments at the beginning of college. UIC students who joined those departments midway through their college progression were regarded as interlopers. As one student told me, "We would think of UIC as some department far away from the campus, like at the corner of the campus, and they're the minority . . . They have to come to our department to listen to the courses given by our professors."

Alongside perceptions of foreignness were also perceptions of inferior academic ability. Another student used notable phrases to describe UIC students, describing them as "lacking seriousness" while again pitting them against "native" students like himself. These negative perceptions were only reinforced by the college's higher tuition that was double that of other parts of the university. In fact, the double tuition became a particular flashpoint when UIC first opened in 2006. At the time, all students faced significant increases in tuition, but the Student Council singled out UIC for its notably higher sticker price as the symbolic representative of academic capitalism against which all other students could protest. These early renderings of UIC solidified perceptions of the college as an expensive playground for students with financial means. Though the protests have long dissipated, the framing of UIC students as affluent, internationally mobile, and undeserving of entry into Yonsei continue to circulate among students.

While these student dynamics may be but small matters relative to the many advantages UIC bestows, they are indicative of the contradictions of an international college that relies on recruiting South Korean citizens. Yonsei maintains arbitrary structural separations that prop up UIC, like a separate campus location and higher tuition, in order to justify the specialness of an international college within the larger university, even though it is unclear whether UIC students are actually different from the majority student body upon entering. This creates a contentious learning environment for these students, who are also South Korean citizens but nonetheless ostracized for their perceived foreignness. More broadly, these tensions underscore how profoundly institutional priorities can shape not just students' international trajectories but their very experiences on campus.

Audrey and Yuri: Illegitimate Elites

Audrey and Yuri became close friends during college, an unlikely pairing between two very different individuals that may not have happened but for UIC. A transnational returnee from Turkey and a local student from Seoul, these young women with different educational backgrounds were transformed by the institution in which they enrolled. One such way was through the language that they spoke with each other, in which Korean and English were used interchangeably, a form of bilingual code-switching. I noticed this unique way of speaking during my conversations with Audrey and Yuri, whom I met together. While I asked questions in English, they interjected Korean words or phrases within their English responses, or fluidly switched between Korean and English when reflecting upon information with one another. This manner of speaking rouses concepts like hybridity and Third Space, which can describe multilingual interactions in many postcolonial contexts. At UIC, the creation of an American liberal arts college within a South Korean university creates a Third Space of hybrid linguistic practices among students.[37] Yuri explained how this particular way of speaking has become the signature mark of UIC students.

> We look Korean, right? But we don't really speak Korean, or we mix the two. When we mix it, it's very fluent. A lot of the UIC students, they have American experience, or they went to international school or American high school or whatever. So we're more or less Americanized, the atmosphere itself. So I think Yonsei students think of us as undefinable.

Indeed, this unique mix of Korean and English further reinforced perceptions of foreignness of UIC students to those outside the college. The irony is that not everyone who used this distinctly UIC language was a transnational returnee, like Audrey; it was also a learned language through which students who did not spend much time overseas, like Yuri, were able to relate to their UIC peers who had.

These hodgepodge friendships are perhaps what most profoundly shaped the student experience at UIC while further separating the students from those outside the college. When Yuri joined a student club in her freshman year that was mixed with students from across Yonsei, she felt alienated by them despite the many similarities they shared.

> I joined the literature club, and I also did volunteer group. I felt more comfortable, I think, because they all went through similar things when they were in high school as I did . . . [but] they were like, "Whoa, so you're from UIC? I've never seen one. You must speak really good English." They also told me that it sometimes feels awkward to see UIC students hanging out.

More than frivolous interactions, these student experiences matter because they reflect both UIC students' agency in forging new communities within an experimental learning space alongside their exclusion from established social spaces within the larger university. And as students negotiated their ambiguous status as South Korean citizens but nonetheless "foreigners" within Yonsei, they faced very real consequences.

One such consequence was their marginalization from departmental networks, which may have repercussions for their career prospects. Though UIC students eventually join a department upon declaring a major and become graduates of that department, their departmental ties were much more diffuse than for other students. UIC students were caught in an awkward middle: they never quite entered the fold of their adoptive department because they were regarded as interlopers; they also never quite formed a robust UIC network because of the expectation that they join another department. When I asked Audrey what she thought of the other students in the political science department that she joined when she declared her major, she told me,

> UIC is fairly new, and [political science] has been around for a long time. Even within Yonsei, it's a very strong department. If people say, "I'm a Yonsei [political science] major," they immediately

know, "Wow, this kid is smart." I think that the students have that pride. They know that they've earned that because they're just at the top of their peers. Definitely, they have this sense of pride in their identity as a Yonsei [political science] department. You can see that. Whereas UIC identity . . .

Audrey trailed off. Her statement reveals the complex identification that UIC students had in relation to their departmental peers. It isn't that UIC students lacked from the global positioning that their college provided them, but that same globality also signaled that they did not legitimately belong within what was presumably their departmental home.

Today, UIC bears little resemblance to the intimate liberal arts college founded over a decade ago. It now spans three divisions that offer sixteen majors taught by 106 faculty members to more than 2,500 students, making it one of the largest colleges at Yonsei.[38] Amid this spectacular growth, students have raised concerns over the college's lack of clear institutional identity as UIC struggles to keep its class sizes small and adds new majors that have little to do with the liberal arts.[39] While the university may tout UIC's curricular additions and growing student body as indicative of its success, even well-positioned students like Audrey see this as the source of their illegitimacy. She told me,

Along with the newness is that we're still establishing our identity, and we're trying to establish that *within* Yonsei. So it's not just how others view us and how they accept us . . . but also how we see ourselves and how much we want to be a part of it . . . There are so many changes going on that I feel that UIC is losing its uniqueness. It's losing its identity. It doesn't know what UIC is. I don't know what UIC is. What are we? Are we really focusing on liberal arts? Are we *just* a college that is for English instruction so *any* major that teaches in English can be part of UIC? What exactly is it anymore? I don't know because every year there are so many changes going on. I feel like the dean and the professors are still just experimenting with this and trying to see what's successful, what's not. But for the students, I've already graduated. It causes a lot of confusion.

Audrey's and Yuri's experiences reflect how the ambiguous institutional positioning of the college is tied to the students' feelings of dislocation on campus.

Summary

Asian universities have adopted the American liberal arts model to meet international standards of excellence and attract more students. Amid a domestic student shortage in South Korea and government policies that try to ameliorate this, Yonsei launched an American-style liberal arts college in order to position itself as a provider of global knowledge that will attract international students. It has done so by aggressively adopting the American liberal arts model to create a distinct space of learning in the form of an international college from which it can also profit. Contrary to its stated mission, however, UIC does not necessarily attract international students but instead recruits primarily domestic students who possess English fluency and other forms of global cultural capital. Yonsei has, in effect, repurposed an international college to meet the needs of globally minded domestic students. But the many contradictions of the college—between its all-American veneer and its primarily South Korean student body, between its global rhetoric and its remote location in Songdo, between its higher tuition and its marginal status within the larger university—have created a fraught environment for its students, who encounter perceptions of foreignness despite their domestic citizenship.

Two of those students are Audrey and Yuri, who are both South Korean citizens but with quite different educational backgrounds upon entering UIC. Because the college created artificial structural separations that forced such different students together, these two students formed a close bond, in no small part due to their shared experiences as students of an experimental college as well as a byproduct of their social exclusion by other students across Yonsei. They were both acutely aware of how their affiliation with an international college became a proxy for their globality, which simultaneously transformed them into illegitimate members within Yonsei and cosmopolitan elites within South Korea. Their story shows how a South Korean university's contradictory efforts to expand into global student markets can shape students' experiences in very real ways.

4
The Contradictions of Choice

To go abroad or not? It's a question that many South Korean students ask themselves as they weigh their college options. While the previous two chapters explored how universities create new pathways for internationally mobile students, this chapter tells the story of the young men and women who made the choice to enter into them. These students may be studying at universities on opposite sides of the world, but their experiences display unexpected parallels.

Indeed, unconventional institutional arrangements across Berkeley and Seoul give South Korean students an array of choices in pursuing higher learning abroad or at home. This chapter begins with the question of choice. Showcasing students who aspired to attend UC Berkeley or Yonsei University, I investigate the choice each student made in selecting a university. Young and mobile, these students typify the millennial generation's education exodus out of South Korea, where overseas study is normalized from an early age. Perhaps more so than students from any other country, South Korean students have become the ultimate flexible citizens as they are presented with a wide range of transnational education options abroad or at home that have become part of their student experience. But what is less clear is how students made the choices that they did amid the realities they faced. Often a student's "choice" to study abroad or not was constrained by a lack of choices in alternative directions. And this raises important questions about how we frame the choices that students make and how we define the flexibility of the students who make those choices.

In this chapter, I show how the pursuit of higher learning abroad or at home is not necessarily a proactive choice but rather an accumulation of life circumstances and calculations upon which universities capitalize. I begin by outlining the realities of the South Korean education system with its rigid college preparatory tracks. Amid ongoing liberalization of this system, gaining admission into college has become much more expensive and cutthroat for students and their parents. Still, a college education is essential to attaining, or even just maintaining, middle-class status for South Korean students. But with opportunities to pursue higher learning in Berkeley and Seoul through unconventional pathways, students are now presented with alternative means to educational success and economic prosperity.

I then present ethnographic vignettes of four students from across the class spectrum who made the "choice" to enter either a community college in California or an international college in South Korea as an alternative route into the more selective institutions of UC Berkeley or Yonsei. These four students narrate their choices that could lead to an elite university while acknowledging the realities that made their choices possible.

Choices as Alternatives

One day every November, half a million South Korean students wake up at the first light of dawn to take the College Scholastic Ability Test, also known as the suneung. The entire country holds its breath on this day: businesses close, the stock market opens late, planes are grounded, military drills pause, and parents pray for their children's success. The Day of Silence, as exam day is also known, may be only nine hours long, but the students who take the national college entrance exam have been preparing for it for many grueling years. The exam measures students' abilities across a wide range of subjects, including Korean, English, history, math, and foreign languages, which are based on the South Korean high school national curriculum. Their intense preparations culminate on this one day, which will determine the university into which students can gain admission, which in turn has an enormous influence in determining their future economic prospects.

Suffice it to say that the pressure to perform well is immense. While exams have been part of the country's education system since dynastic rule, the particular pressure around the college entrance exam is a more recent development. The Park Chung Hee regime, in its campaign to industrialize South Korea, abolished the middle school entrance exam in 1971 and then the high school entrance exam in 1974 in order to expand access to secondary education. The college entrance exam remained intact, however, which marked the beginning of its reputation as the "one-chance exam" that would determine a South Korean student's future. Then in 1980, shortly after the assassination of Park Chung Hee, the subsequent military government banned universities from administering their own entrance exam and instead introduced a national exam for all college-bound students, in large part to exert more control over universities that were involved in the pro-democracy movement against military rule.

Today, the exam still remains an integral part of the South Korean education system. For several decades, the exam was the only way that students could gain admission into universities, and preparing for the exam was seen as a rite of passage into adulthood. More than just another standardized test, it determines which schools students are even eligible to apply to based on their score. A student's university, in turn, opens up job opportunities through tightly knit alumni networks that help usher in younger peers from the same school, both in the short term and over the course of a lifetime. And over the decades, the responsibility of preparing students for the exam has shifted from the state to the market, or more aptly from teachers to parents, spurred by the burgeoning of South Korea's shadow education market and economic austerity measures put in place after the Asian financial crisis of 1997.

Following the Asian financial crisis, the South Korean government also implemented a series of policies that allowed universities more autonomy in determining their own admissions criteria as the country's leadership sought to shed remnants of South Korea's authoritarian past. This liberalization in admissions gave rise to the popularity of special admissions (susi), beginning in 2002, as an alternative to regular admissions (jeongsi). While regular admissions places heavy emphasis on a student's college entrance exam score, special admissions allows students to forgo the exam altogether in favor of one of several admissions tracks each administered by an individual school. These tracks typically consider a student's high school records, extracurricular activities, volunteer service, recommendation letters, interviews, essays, and special abilities in foreign languages or sports.

The rise of special admissions further fueled the popularity of early study abroad as a way to prepare South Korean youth for the English language skills demanded by this new system. It also led to the rapid increase of foreign language high schools that systematically prepare students for the system's specific entry requirements. Today, the majority of incoming university students in South Korea arrive through special admissions, especially at the most selective schools. While this new system has certainly relieved pressures around the college entrance exam, it has also created a host of new pressures for students to accumulate desirable skills and experiences that will give them a competitive edge in the admissions process. After all, early study abroad, mastery of foreign languages, competitive internships, novel extracurricular activities, and eso-teric sports all demand the careful planning and family resources arguably much greater than those demanded by exam preparation.

Yet the rules of educational success in South Korea are hardly steadfast. In 2019 Minister of Justice Cho Kuk came under fire when it was revealed that his daughter was falsely listed as the primary author of a research article published in a scientific journal that helped her gain entry into a selective university through special admissions. Shortly after Cho's disgraceful resignation, a govern-mental audit exposed dozens of cases of universities admitting chil-dren of professors under similarly dubious circumstances, sparking outrage among students and parents. Since then, under a banner of rooting out corruption and systemic inequities, the government has vowed to reduce the proportion of students that universities are allowed to admit through special admissions while reinforcing regular admissions as the primary method of entry with a series of policies that are currently unfolding.

It is against this backdrop of a constantly shifting neoliberal educa-tion market, with its less codified rules and more costly demands, that South Korean students and their families engage in the admissions process. Liberalization has only further reinforced the hypercompeti-tive tracks, whether via regular or special admissions, as the only via-ble routes to a prosperous life in South Korea. Indeed, scholars have noted that the South Korean education system remains exception-ally rigid in its inability to afford students alternative pathways to economic success, even with the expansion of alternative education opportunities.[1] And at a time when youth unemployment is rampant, a student's education pedigree is crucial to attaining upward socio-economic mobility, or even just avoiding downward socioeconomic mobility. But for South Korean students who may not want to navigate such a rigid system, an alternative pathway is exactly what they seek.

This is where higher education reform efforts across Berkeley and Seoul intersect with South Korean students' educational endeavors.

Alternative pathways into UC Berkeley or Yonsei offer students an opportunity to exit, or otherwise bypass, a rigid system in which the only options are to undergo exhaustive exam preparations or to accumulate costly "specs" deemed worthy of admission to a selective university.[2] What follows are the stories of four students who pursued an alternative pathway in different ways. I highlight these particular individuals because they each deliberated over the choice to leave South Korea or the choice to stay, each choice shaped by a relative lack of choices in alternative directions.

Jihun: The Choice to Leave

I opened chapter 2 with a vignette of an aspiring film major enrolled at a community college near Berkeley. In 2016 Jihun was finishing his first year at Diablo Valley College, a community college located thirty minutes east in Pleasant Hill, when we met at the swanky café inside the Berkeley Art Museum and Pacific Film Archive. He and I, along with his mother, chatted over espressos and light lunch fare. It was his mother who initially suggested that the three of us meet so that she could introduce me to her son. I knew Jihun's mother, Yeongju, through my work at UC Berkeley's Center for Korean Studies, where she was affiliated as a visiting scholar while on a sabbatical from her position as a research librarian at a government institute in South Korea. She brought her two sons with her; her husband stayed in South Korea, where he was a professor.

This was neither Jihun's nor his mother's first time living in the United States. They, along with Jihun's younger brother, moved to upstate New York for two years a decade earlier, while Jihun's father stayed in South Korea. Back then, Yeongju was a graduate student in library sciences at SUNY Buffalo while Jihun and his younger brother were in elementary school. The culture shock they experienced in Buffalo was challenging, particularly for Yeongju. She described how difficult it was to overcome language barriers and make friends in her graduate program. Harsh winters in Buffalo did not agree with her, either. Jihun also faced his own personal challenges, but as an adaptable young child, he was much quicker to acculturate to American life and learn English, which benefited him tremendously when he returned to the United States this second time around as a college student at Diablo Valley.

This multigenerational crisscrossing over the Pacific Ocean was a commonly shared experience I encountered among the South Korean students whom I met studying in California. Many of the students shared how they first came to the United States for early study abroad with one or both of their parents, who brought their children over while pursuing a corporate expat assignment or an academic sabbatical in the United States. In fact, the Center for Korean Studies hosts a visiting scholar program that was often used for this exact purpose. The program enables foreign scholars like Yeongju to affiliate for up to two years while sponsored on a J exchange visa. Most visiting scholars who are affiliated with the Center come from South Korea, and nearly all whose sabbatical I oversaw used the opportunity to bring their children with them for early study abroad as they pursued their own professional activities at UC Berkeley.

After completing his last two years of elementary school in Buffalo, Jihun returned to South Korea with his mother and brother to begin middle school. In middle school South Korean youth are expected to become much more serious about their studies as they begin the intense preparations for college admission, what many South Koreans characterize as "education fever."[3] But after his relatively more relaxed school years in the American system, Jihun was not well prepared for the rigid expectations that awaited him upon reentering the South Korean system, a predicament in which many early study abroad returnees find themselves. This situation has become so commonplace that, beginning in 2016, the South Korean government mandated that all early study abroad returnees who have spent at least two years overseas pass a reentry exam in order to reenroll into the grade that corresponds with their age. Jihun undertook his early study abroad before this policy was introduced, but he, too, fell behind in school.

By the time Jihun was in high school, he was hopelessly behind his more competitive peers, especially in math and science. He described his lackluster academic performance as his mother added some commentary.

Jihun: I didn't study hard.

Yeongju: He did not like high school because in Korea, many students study hard to go to college. They study hard from early in the morning to late at night. But he did not like that. I think he had the ability for language and writing, but in the Korean system, all students need to be good at all subjects. But he was not. He liked writing and music. So he didn't like studying in high school very much.

Jihun: I was not trying hard enough. Once you don't really study, you kind of get left behind by teachers. And obviously, I was one of them. It was not bad, but it was not good. It was just high school.

In his last year of high school, Jihun applied to a few selective universities in South Korea but was not admitted. His mother then swiftly arranged her visiting scholar appointment at UC Berkeley and moved to the Bay Area with her two sons. Jihun enrolled at Diablo Valley, and his younger brother enrolled at a nearby middle school for a second round of early study abroad.

Though Jihun described himself as a listless and unmotivated student throughout high school, he transformed into an academically engaged one at Diablo Valley. He waxed eloquent about his courses, which were on subjects that he actually enjoyed and gave him ample opportunity to explore his passion and interests. He talked enthusiastically about how his classes at Diablo Valley had a much more open atmosphere that encouraged him to share his views on a wide range of topics, even on ones that are socially taboo in South Korea, like same-sex marriage and recreational drug use. He took a media studies course in his first semester and discovered that he loved learning about film. With his newfound enthusiasm for school, he invested a lot more time and energy into his academic life and even joined the science club, a place where he could easily meet other international students from South Korea. His goal was to do well in his classes at Diablo Valley and then transfer to UC Berkeley.

Jihun is another example of a South Korean student finding an alternative route to academic success through California's community colleges. His choice to study in the United States stems from his desire to seek out the global promise of an American education just as much as it stems from the rigidity of the South Korean education system that does not allow room for deviation, especially for late bloomers like Jihun. Indeed, many students who do not meet the exacting requirements for admission into a selective university in South Korea are left with few choices. Even Jessica, the remarkably driven and focused student who attended De Anza College before transferring to UC Berkeley whom I introduced in chapter 2, vaguely mentioned that she "had no choice" but to go abroad when it came time to apply to college, implying that she was likely not a competitive candidate for the top band of schools in South Korea. But California community colleges allow students like Jihun and Jessica to prove themselves as the academically talented students that they are and set their sights toward selective universities like UC Berkeley.

In this way, Jihun's story is less a counterexample to Jessica's but rather a reflection of the limited range of choices these students were presented with as they took stock of their situation and enrolled in a community college. On one hand, Jessica and her family proactively chose California after they consulted with an education agent, who recommended this admissions pathway for Jessica's particular needs and abilities. Jihun's situation is different, but he and Jessica nonetheless shared the same hopes and anxieties about their future. He, like many other South Korean students, was pushed out of the hypercompetitive admissions tracks into a South Korean university that would provide him with a reasonable chance at middle-class status. While this left him with little choice but to exit the competition, his prior early study abroad experience and his mother's educational savvy offered him a second chance in California.

Yeongju understood all of this as she managed her son's application to Diablo Valley alongside her visiting scholar appointment. She expressed a genuine appreciation for her son's unique traits and abilities and was especially proud of Jihun for discovering his passion for film. But she knew this was in stark contrast to what is generally expected of South Korean mothers, who are supposed to carve out a pathway for their children's educational success in South Korea and equip them with the academic credentials that will help them face an even more competitive job market in their adult lives.[4] With resignation, Yeongju described her own failings as a mother.

> So in Korea, I am kind of a failure. Failed mother. Because he didn't go to college in Korea. So I'm kind of a loser in Korea. But I don't mind because I trust him. Because he has talent in specific ways, specific areas. In Korea, he was not accepted. But in America, everything is okay. I like it very much. If he likes living here, I like it.

Her comments reveal how she internalized the "burden of self-development," in which women must disproportionately take responsibility for their children's success, defined by labor market outcomes.[5] While Yeongju was certainly not under the false impression that life in the United States guaranteed economic success, she found comfort in Jihun's academic accomplishments in an environment that allowed him to thrive and that opened a door to further advancement. Such advancement, she acknowledged, could also pave the way for Jihun's triumphant return to South Korea should he wish to do so.

I highlight Jihun's trajectory because his story represents a recurring one that I encountered among the South Korean students who had entered the community college pipeline. Jihun and others left South Korea in pursuit of the promise of a blank slate in California.

They were equally squeezed out of South Korea's unforgiving college admissions tracks just as much as they "chose" to study in California, each student's story reflecting a different gradation of choice. Meanwhile, the choices that students made were only possible because of their prior early study abroad experience and English fluency. In Jihun's case, the intelligence, determination, and educational status of his mother also contributed to his international mobility. At the same time, as we saw in chapter 2, the confluence of budget constraints and legislative changes have pressured California community colleges to open their doors to more international students in the last decade. Indeed, the choice to enter into the community college pipeline is born of an unconventional marriage between the mobile trajectories of South Korean youth and the dramatic higher education reforms implemented in California following the Great Recession. But such a union begs another question: What happens to students who deviate from the prescribed admissions tracks but choose not to leave South Korea?

Seunghui: The Choice to Stay

I met Seunghui in 2012 during my research year at Yonsei. At the time we met, she was a college senior majoring in political science. Worldly and well-traveled, she shared with me the early experiences that cultivated her cosmopolitan outlook. She spent three years of elementary school in the United States for early study abroad when her father's job at a South Korean multinational company enabled him to bring the whole family to the United States. She also took trips to Japan and throughout Europe during her childhood. She furthered her English proficiency in high school when she studied at the Hankuk Academy of Foreign Studies, a foreign language high school in Yongin.[6] Following her parents' hopes for her to become a diplomat, she originally intended to go to college in the

United States and studied in her high school's international track, which offers instruction entirely in English and a rigorous schedule of Advanced Placement courses. But the global financial crisis unfolded during her high school years and abruptly changed her family's financial situation—and her plans to go abroad.

Seunghui's turnaround from US-bound to not reflects a broader downturn that the global financial crisis created for outbound student mobility from South Korea. The number of South Korean students enrolled in US colleges and universities peaked at over seventy-five thousand in the 2008–2009 academic year, but that number has dropped by 33 percent as of the 2019–2020 academic year, even before the pandemic exacerbated the downturn even further.[7] The same downward trend can be found among South Korean students who pursue early study abroad. The number of South Korean students who pursued early study abroad peaked at over twenty-seven thousand in 2007, but since then that number has dropped sharply by 68 percent as of 2019.[8] While the reasons for this downturn are multitudinous and complex, the global financial crisis has certainly dampened South Korean students' willingness to study overseas as their families tighten their belts and reconsider the financial and emotional costs that overseas education demands.

While Seunghui's classmates headed off to the United States, she searched for an alternative way to attend college in South Korea. Her high school curriculum had not prepared her for either regular or special admissions, which left her with few choices, she told me.

> Well, I actually was part of the English department in my high school. That English department prepared for college abroad, so all my classmates actually studied the SAT and the APs to go to the United States for college. I also did that, too, but I ended up choosing to stay in Korea because of financial reasons. I wasn't really prepared to go abroad. So, all I had was SAT scores and AP scores, right? But you have to take the national examination to go to a Korean school. But departments like UIC don't require that

> national exam score. So, this was pretty much one of the few places
> that I could actually apply for because I wanted to stay in Korea.

She was able to enter Yonsei as a student at Underwood International College (UIC). At roughly $12,000 per year, UIC tuition was significantly cheaper than what an international student would pay at most universities in the United States, where Seunghui would also incur costly living expenses. In fact, UIC prominently touts its cheaper tuition compared to universities in the United States, as opposed to its higher tuition compared to the rest of Yonsei, as a way to advertise itself as an attractive alternative to US-bound students like Seunghui.

As I discussed in chapter 3, UIC also served as a catchall destination for South Korean students who sought admission into a selective university in South Korea through unconventional means. Like Seunghui, a number of students whom I met had been preparing to go abroad to the United States but changed course for one reason or another. Equipped with only their SAT and Advanced Placement exam scores, they had little choice but to enter an American-style college like UIC that would accept them on that basis. Others, like Yuri, whom I also introduced in chapter 3, never intended to go abroad at all but were drawn to the college's liberal arts curriculum as well as its affiliation with a selective university in South Korea. In fact, Yuri even mentioned that her first choice was to study in the art history department at Seoul National University, an even more selective university than Yonsei, but that she did not gain admission there. She accepted her offer at UIC, both because of its unique curricular offerings and because it served as a strategic admissions pathway into Yonsei.

In this way, UIC presents both a novel choice and a de facto alternative for students like Seunghui and Yuri. They sought out an international college as much for its American-style curriculum as they did because their prior education positioned them at an advantage to enter. On the one hand, Yuri gained admission into a selective university in South Korea by studying in an experimental learning environment that intrigued her. Her first choice may have been to join a traditional department at an even more selective university, but she still found a great opportunity at Yonsei that capitalized on her English fluency and preparation at a foreign language high school. On the other, Seunghui had wanted to go abroad for a long time. Her rigorous high school curriculum prepared her to do so but also precluded her from entering a South Korean university through the typical avenues. When life circumstances unexpectedly changed her plans, the rigidly prescribed admissions tracks in South Korea left her with few options. But UIC offered her the American-style learning environment for which she had been preparing as well as an alternative means through which to attend a selective university in South Korea. These two students may have had different motivations, but the comparable ways they arrived at UIC reflect the limited choices they were presented with as each made a calculated decision to enter a novel pathway into a selective university without having to leave South Korea.

Seunghui's high school education prepared her well for UIC. She thrived in the common curriculum courses, which emphasized reading and writing and encouraged an open atmosphere of discussion where students could freely articulate their viewpoints. In her second year, she selected political science as her major because she was drawn to the strong reputation of the political science department. Once she started taking courses in the department, however, she found that they were not as engaging or deep as she had hoped, in large part because of their mode of delivery. The courses she took within the political science department were all taught in English, but unlike at UIC, the professors who taught them were not all comfortable teaching courses in that language, she told me. As Yonsei has adopted aggressive internationalization reforms that reverberate beyond UIC, even traditional departments have converted a sizable proportion of their courses into English. But Seunghui felt that the professors with the most seniority and experience were not the ones who were teaching those courses and instead delegated them to junior faculty members or adjuncts. When I asked her why she didn't take courses taught in Korean with more senior faculty members, her answer surprised me.

Seunghui: It's very disappointing that we don't get to have all the good professors because some just don't teach for UIC students . . . The depth of knowledge that we deal with in class is much more deep in the political science classes conducted in Korean rather than English.

Me: Was there a reason why you didn't take those Korean-taught classes?

Seunghui: Because I've been studying in English since high school, so I feel more comfortable with English when it comes to academic writing and reading. I wasn't really sure whether I would do well in the Korean classes, although I'm comfortable in Korean speaking.

Though Seunghui is a fluent Korean speaker born and raised in Seoul, she had been taking academic coursework primarily in English since high school within an exclusive curriculum that prepared students to go abroad. Her subsequent education at UIC allowed her to continue learning in an all-English environment. So by the time she entered the political science department at Yonsei, she felt unprepared for advanced coursework in Korean. Conversation in Korean may have been easy for Seunghui, but academic reading and writing were not. And Seunghui was not unusual in this regard. The majority of the UIC students whom I met, who indicated that they were also fluent Korean speakers, told me that they still did not feel comfortable taking college courses in Korean for similar reasons.

Despite her language limitations, Seunghui excelled in her major courses and was active in her department. She was elected as the class representative for UIC students majoring in political science and used her position to try to improve relations between UIC students and traditional students in the political science department.

She organized cocurricular events and brought forth salient issues to the biweekly meetings of the UIC student council. Meanwhile, she was preparing her graduate school applications to finally pursue her dream of attending an American university. She eschewed her parents' hopes for her to become a diplomat and instead set her sights on becoming a scholar of political science. She did, however, feel anxious that her language limitations and lack of meaningful relationships to senior faculty members in the political science department at Yonsei might have repercussions for her academic career should she want return to South Korea after her doctoral studies abroad. Nonetheless, she recognized how well positioned her UIC education made her for graduate study in the United States and threw herself into preparing her applications.

I highlight Seunghui's trajectory because her story represents a recurring one that I encountered among the South Korean students who entered UIC as an alternative admissions pathway into a South Korean university. Seunghui and others arrived at UIC for a variety of reasons, but the commonality that they shared is that they capitalized on their existing forms of global cultural capital to gain entry into a selective university in South Korea. Their "choice" to attend UIC was actually a strategic maneuver that reflects the limited range of choices each student weighed against the hypercompetitive college admissions system in South Korea. Meanwhile, that choice was only possible because institutions like Yonsei are capitalizing on the various forms of globality that South Korean students potentially bring as they adopt American standards of excellence in their pursuit of institutional prestige, as we saw in chapter 3. Indeed, such a choice is shaped out of the complex interplay of aspiration and anxiety held by both South Korean students and the universities that they attend. Yet if even relatively well-to-do students like Seunghui face a limited range of choices, what happens to students who are not as advantaged?

Taeho: The Illusion of Choice

Taeho and I met in 2016 at a trendy coffee shop and bakery that had just opened near the UC Berkeley campus. We were lucky to find an empty table at the end of the spring semester when students were busy studying for their final exams. Despite his own busy schedule, Taeho took some time to meet me during his study week before he would take his last set of final exams and graduate from UC Berkeley.

Graduating from UC Berkeley was certainly a momentous achievement for Taeho, a first-generation college student from Seoul. While South Korea boasts of the world's highest rate of higher education attainment among youth, this is a recent phenomenon that cuts differently across generations. Today, 70 percent of twenty-five- to thirty-four-year-olds in South Korea have attained higher education, but only 25 percent of fifty-five- to sixty-four-year-olds in South Korea have—the starkest difference between parent and child generations among member countries of the Organisation for Economic Co-operation and Development (OECD).[9] In other words, South Korean millennials are the most educated in the world, but their parents are certainly not. Taeho is one of those millennials.

Over iced coffee and baked goods, Taeho told me about the trajectory that led him to UC Berkeley. His father was one of eight siblings and came from Jeolla Province. His mother was one of seven siblings and came from Chungcheong Province. They never attended college and moved to Seoul, where his father found work as an interior designer and where Taeho and his younger sister were born. Taeho grew up in Seoul and graduated from a public high school in 2007. He had wanted to attend Konkuk University, a private university in Seoul, because it was close to his home, but his college entrance exam score was too low. He didn't know what else to do, so he spent a whole year not doing much of anything—"drinking with friends," he told me bemusedly—before he began his compulsory military service in South Korea. While most South Korean men begin their military service after completing a couple of years of college, if not after finishing college entirely, Taeho simply went straight away since he wasn't enrolled in school.

It was during these two years of conscription when Taeho decided to become more serious about his future. He began to study for the entrance exam again, but his military friends gave him a different idea. Some of these friends had completed college already in the United States and had returned to South Korea to complete their own compulsory military service. They told him about the abundant higher education opportunities in the United States, including community colleges, which opened up a new set of possibilities for Taeho.

> I had time to think about my future. So I was thinking seriously for my future. Then I decided to study, again, for the Korean version of SAT at first. While I'm studying there, some of my friends in there came from America. They were also yuhaksaeng [international students] from Korea to have military service. They recommend me to come study in America. They said it's easier to get into university than in Korea. Because if I studied in Korea, I have to *really* study a lot for the Korean version of SAT. But it's relatively easier [in America]. That's what they said. So anyway, I decided to come. I started to study English.

Yet Taeho's English skills were not strong enough for college in the United States. He told me that he could not even utter a single sentence in English at the time. South Korean students may study English as part of their general curriculum, but this is insufficient preparation for college-level coursework. Taeho had not had the advantages of extramural classes or private tutors, let alone the specialized curriculum of a foreign language high school or early study abroad opportunities. In fact, Taeho had never even traveled outside of South Korea. His parents, whom he described as honest and kind "country people," knew very little about navigating study abroad opportunities for their children. But Taeho was undeterred. He stumbled upon a brochure for a language school in Southern California that showcased a beautiful photograph of its building next to the

Pacific Ocean. He had made his decision. Once he was discharged from the military, he packed his bags and moved to Los Angeles.

Taeho was a fast learner. Upon completing a year of intensive English at his language school in San Pedro, he enrolled at Santa Monica College, primarily because it was close to his language school. Incidentally, Santa Monica has the largest international student population among California community colleges. He befriended other international students from South Korea, many of whom he described as "having some money" but not serious about their studies. Unlike them, he took his studies seriously because he had come on his own accord and not from any parental pressure, he told me. During the day, he took a wide range of classes and was drawn to the sciences. Biology intrigued him the most, but chemistry was less demanding of English, so he took classes in biochemistry. In the evenings and on weekends, he worked, illegally, at a restaurant in the Koreatown neighborhood of Los Angeles or as a caterer for weddings. After three years studying at Santa Monica College while paying his way through odd jobs, he finished his coursework with a 4.0 grade point average and the intention to transfer to a UC school as a chemistry major.

Taeho began as what the journalist Jeff Selingo describes as a "passenger," a student who approaches the college admissions process without a definitive understanding of the larger implications of his choices.[10] The choices he made and the ways he made them were often the result of advice from the people around him or of chance encounters. As a first-generation college student, he navigated the college admissions process mostly on his own, which resulted in a lack of information and missed opportunities. His parents were nonetheless supportive of his decisions and even helped him financially to the extent that they could. And over time, Taeho became more confident and more savvy, less like a "passenger" and more like a "driver." He knew that his grade point average made him a competitive transfer applicant. Though most students who transfer from Santa Monica go to UCLA because of its proximity, something that Taeho might have done earlier, this time he set his sights for something different.

> My goal was just Berkeley. So actually, I didn't want to apply to any UC except Berkeley. I was thinking of just applying to Berkeley, but my friends say that you should apply to some others, just in case. I was so confident because my GPA was 4.0 for three years . . . I was so confident. I must get in. (laughs) So anyway, I got into Berkeley.

Once at UC Berkeley, however, Taeho encountered a new set of challenges. He described large classes of hundreds of students taught by professors who only cared about research and didn't care much about teaching, a stark contrast to the smaller classes he enjoyed at his community college in Santa Monica. He struggled in classes that demanded more English, especially when the class sizes were large. He sought out help from the Student Learning Center, but he found the experience agitating. He began to rely on websites like RateMy-Professors.com to navigate which classes to take so as to avoid those that required more writing assignments. And though he appreciated UC Berkeley's beautiful campus, he was disturbed by the extreme income disparity and inflated living costs in the surrounding neighborhoods of East Bay.

Roughly a quarter of students at UC Berkeley are estimated to be first-generation college students, meaning that their parents did not graduate from college. Their unique challenges have been well documented, particularly for those who arrive at selective schools and must navigate a new academic setting without the same cultural capital that their more privileged peers have.[11] In response, institutions have set up mentoring services and other resources to help these students succeed and graduate. But while recognizing that first-generation students are not all homogenous, most colleges and universities treat these students as a distinct population from international students, who are assumed to have different needs. Indeed, at UC Berkeley, the resources intended to help first-generation students are housed in an entirely separate office and campus location from its transition programs for international students.

Taeho had no idea that his university offered special resources for first-generation students like himself. As he had done before, he relied on himself to figure things out, and eventually, he settled into his new campus. He found a room to rent in a house in South Berkeley for $800 a month and rode his bike to school each day. He made friends in various student clubs and within the broader Korean student community. He also joined a study group with other community college transfers majoring in chemistry. But as a nontraditional student nearing the age of thirty, Taeho was considerably older than his traditional college-aged peers. He spent most of his free time visiting his girlfriend, who still lived in Los Angeles.

When I asked him about his plans after his upcoming graduation, Taeho told me that he was going to work as a research assistant in a chemistry lab at UC Berkeley for a year while preparing his graduate school applications for a PhD program in chemistry in the United States. He sounded excited about the research that he was about to undertake, which was a continuation of what he had done in his last semester as an undergraduate doing lab work in advanced organic chemistry. Though he had ambiguous feelings about his Berkeley education, he did make a point to highlight how invaluable it was to gain lab experience as an undergraduate, something that would not have been possible at Santa Monica College. He enjoyed the applied nature of lab work and wanted to continue in this direction. He did, however, admit to me that he really wanted to go to medical school or another professional health school. But given the high tuition of medical school and limited financial aid availability for international students, Taeho felt that he had little choice but to pursue a research career. Attending a doctoral program would likely provide him with tuition benefits and a living stipend. Meanwhile, his girlfriend, also an international student from South Korea, would no longer be eligible to stay in the United States after graduating from college, which would likely lead to the end of their relationship.

I highlight Taeho's trajectory because his story exemplifies an extreme example in which study abroad is no longer a choice but a "voluntary exile."[12] While study abroad is often depicted as a privileged choice, Taeho chose to study abroad because he faced a distinct lack of opportunities within the bottom tier of South Korea's highly stratified education system. The "choices" he made—to move to California, to learn English, to study at Santa Monica College and then UC Berkeley, to major in chemistry instead of biology, to become a researcher instead of a medical professional, even to maintain a relationship with his girlfriend—were not so much proactive decisions but rather the result of his commendable determination coming head-to-head with the structural inequities that he faced. But unlike Jihun or Jessica, Taeho never approached his studies at a community college as a way to reenter South Korea as "a more profitable citizen."[13] In fact, he told me that he had no intention of returning to South Korea and had not even visited once since he moved to California six years earlier.

Taeho came to the United States to stay. Another student whom I met pursued international education as a means to stay in South Korea permanently.

Brandon: Without a Choice

Brandon was one of the first students I met at Yonsei in 2012. He actually reached out to me directly after I sent some inquiries seeking out students to interview through a mutual contact. We met at a coffee shop in the Sinchon area of Seoul to chat about his student experience at UIC. Upon meeting, I was immediately struck by his affable personality, as well as his unquestionably American accent.

Accordingly, he introduced himself to me by his American name rather than the Korean name he was given at birth.

Brandon was born in South Korea but moved with his family to Colorado when he was two years old in the mid-1990s. He told me that his parents were seeking more economic opportunities and eventually just stayed. Though Brandon's family were all South Korean citizens who intended to return to South Korea, they reminded me more of immigrant families who come to the United States without much economic or social capital but with a vague dream of pursuing a better future for their children. Brandon's family moved to Colorado, and he completed all his primary and secondary education by attending local public schools there. When it came time to go to college, however, things got complicated. While leaving certain things unsaid, Brandon revealed to me that his ambiguous residency status in the United States prevented him from attending college there.

> I was accepted into the University of Colorado at Boulder, but since it's a university in the United States, it's expensive. Also, since I was . . . there were some legal complications, and I wasn't exactly . . . a resident in Colorado. I couldn't get the in-state tuition fee, either. So it was really out of our price range.

He then looked to universities in South Korea, where he holds citizenship and where tuition is significantly cheaper than the University of Colorado's nonresident tuition.[14] He told me he enrolled at UIC because an all-English college was really his only option since he hardly spoke any Korean. Meanwhile, his family stayed behind in the United States, though they eventually planned to rejoin him in South Korea.

At first, Brandon was angry about his situation. He left behind his family and friends in the United States to move to a country where he did not speak the language and about which he knew very little. But fortunately, Brandon was gregarious and made new friends easily. He moved into the dormitories at the Yonsei International Campus in Songdo, where he soon found himself living among a community of friends. Most South Korean students who attend Yonsei have a permanent residence in Seoul and resent having to live in the dormitories in the remote location of Songdo, but Brandon enjoyed it very much.

> While we're talking about Songdo, a lot of people say it's not so great and that they didn't have such a great time there, but I want to say that I think it was a good experience for almost everybody, if not everyone there. Because one thing about Songdo is that it created this feeling of community and everyone knew each other . . . Since I didn't really have a home in Korea, I spent my breaks in the dormitory, in Songdo. In a way, I kind of see Songdo as my home. I feel comfortable when I go there, and I know there's always someone I know, friends.

He admitted that being sociable didn't help him focus on his studies, but he came to appreciate his expanded social circle in his new environment. Most of the new friends he made were South Korean. He didn't find too much of a language barrier with them because they were all fluent English speakers, but sometimes his American sensibilities rubbed them the wrong way.

> At first, I was interesting and people wanted to talk to me, but gradually I became weird to them. (laughs) . . . Now I speak Korean, but back then it was kind of hard to speak to me in Korean, so they had a hard time trying to communicate with me. Also, it's a huge culture difference. What kind of jokes were acceptable in the United States are definitely not acceptable here. We're much more reserved. If I want to crack a sexual joke to them, they'll be disgusted here, whereas my other friends would crack up. So it's not much of a language barrier, more of a culture barrier, in terms of students like me.

During our interview, it was fascinating for me to observe how Brandon socially located himself. At times, he referred to other South Korean students as "them" but sometimes switched to "we" when speaking of South Korean students as a whole. He fluctuated between identifying with his South Korean peers and with international students, whose citizenship status he may not have shared but whose struggles in a foreign country he certainly did. Brandon's particular sense of belonging, what the higher education scholar Terrell Strayhorn defines as "students' perceived social support on campus, a feeling or sensation of connectedness, and the experience of mattering," heavily relied on his South Korean citizenship despite that his daily life reflected his experiences as a "foreigner" at Yonsei.[15] For example, he described how holding South Korean citizenship made it easier for him to obtain a cell phone and open a bank account, tasks that were much more complicated for international students. At the same time, he struggled to use the dormitory laundry machines alongside other international students because all the directions were in Korean. He also described how he would use his liminal status to try to influence his South Korean peers to better understand and empathize with the plight of international students.

Indeed, Brandon views his childhood overseas experience as disadvantageous. He imagines that his globality is at odds with his sense of belonging in South Korea. His education in the United States may have provided him with English fluency and an American sense of humor, but it also eroded his social capital within South Korea, so much so that his South Korean peers identified him as "weird." Brandon punctures the stereotype of the glamorous transnational returnee in South Korea. When he moved to Colorado, he lost out on the linguistic and cultural practices of South Korea in order to assimilate into a dominant school curriculum in the United States, a phenomenon known as "subtractive schooling."[16] His accumulation of global cultural capital was accompanied by a systematic separation from other important forms of linguistic and cultural capital, such as proficiency in Korean. Paradoxically, because of his time in the United States, Brandon lacked the full range of educational options that his globality would imply. He arrived at UIC, then, for lack of better choices.

But even someone who seemingly fits the description of the flexible citizen—Audrey, for example, whom I introduced in chapter 3—also had limited Korean language proficiency that shaped her student experience at UIC. Transnational returnees like Audrey often entered UIC as an English language gateway into a South Korean university because they, too, were deficient in the Korean language, a deficiency that was part of their overseas education. Yet these students desired to return to South Korea in their adult lives as a way of reintegrating with their country of citizenship. However, embedded within their professed desire to return were comments implying that their options to stay or go elsewhere were limited. Similar to Brandon, a number of transnational returnees whom I met described limited job prospects or costly tuition in other countries prior to returning to South Korea. Though tuition costs were irrelevant for Audrey, she did admit, after some probing, that she first wanted to attend a liberal arts college in the United States but that she did not gain admission to her first-choice schools there; only then did she consider her options in South Korea that led her to "choose" UIC.

But Brandon never had much of a choice. He described his arrival at UIC as something that was "forced," given his uncertain legal standing in the United States. As he advanced in his studies at UIC, he selected international studies as his major, even though he had very little interest in the subject. His passion was music, he told me, but UIC did not offer music as a major, so he just picked the least unappealing of the other options available. Meanwhile, he continued to foster his musical ambitions by producing his own music videos and sharing them on YouTube. He also joined a hip-hop club, where he could rap and sing with other students. As he pondered life in South Korea beyond college, he would remind himself that any plans would have to wait since he still had to complete his compulsory military service upon graduating.

I highlight Brandon's trajectory because his extreme example illustrates the limited range of choices transnational returnees faced as they negotiated their return to South Korea. The narratives shared by the many transnational returnees whom I met illuminate how their decision to enroll into an international college in South Korea is often the only option because of their deficiency in Korean, calling into question their supposed flexibility. But Brandon's transnational trajectory was never his choice at all. His sojourn from South Korea to the United States and then back to South Korea was never a flexible form of movement and instead was a reflection of his relative lack of choices. And, unlike other transnational returnees, Brandon did not articulate his overseas experience as a source of advantage. It was, to him, the reason for his disconnection to South Korea, the country where he would spend his foreseeable future whether he liked it or not. For Brandon, this much was clear: transnationalism is not always a choice, and international mobility is not always flexible.

Rethinking Flexible Citizenship

In the literature on international student mobility, higher education is often presented as a vast array of choices in a global free marketplace of consumers and providers. This body of work presents cross-border learning less as a cosmopolitan endeavor, as defined by the education scholar Fazal Rizvi, and more as an instrumentalist approach to attaining overseas credentials as a form of material and symbolic capital, as argued by the geographer Johanna Waters.[17] Enterprising youth make strategic choices that serve as "investments in the self to ensure one's forward career progress," often in the frame of advancing into a global future.[18] The flexibility of their movement is deeply intertwined with the flexibility of their educational choices against the backdrop of a neoliberal market logic that produces and reproduces class stratification.[19]

Yet the concept of choice is illusory because it implies that there are viable alternatives. For South Korean students, the choice to pursue higher learning abroad or at home is undertaken against a hyper-competitive college admissions system that is constantly in flux and an increasingly liberalized education sector, where the costs of preparing for college admission are shouldered by students and their parents. While young people know that educational success hardly guarantees economic success, they are also acutely aware that educational failure most definitely leads to economic failure. They call their country "Hell Joseon" to express their hopelessness for a hellish society while nonetheless resigning themselves to educational pressures that may not propel them to prosperity but will at least protect them from extreme poverty. For this reason, students make choices that function primarily to "escape obsolescence" rather than to demonstrate their flexibility in their educational pursuits.[20]

The four students whom I profile in this chapter made such a choice to "escape" their present situations for more promising futures. Their choices were shaped by the extreme rigidity of the South Korean education system that already funneled their choice of college admission into very narrow pathways. But higher education reform efforts made possible alternative routes into selective universities. In California, community colleges were repurposed into an admissions pipeline into UC Berkeley for South Korean students who aspire to attend but may not be admitted right away. In South Korea, UIC was repurposed as an admissions pipeline into Yonsei for globally minded domestic students. These four individuals from across the class spectrum made a choice to pursue higher learning through one of these alternative pathways as they eschewed more established choices where they faced much higher barriers to entry.

For Jihun, the choice to study at Diablo Valley College as a way to enter UC Berkeley was a form of redemption. His lackluster performance in high school precluded his attendance at a selective university in South Korea, but he found a second chance in California. Notably, the opportunity to leave South Korea for California was only possible because of his English fluency as a result of his prior early study abroad experience, as well as his mother's own pursuit of international education. Such an arrangement that allows the professional-managerial class of South Korea to provide study abroad opportunities for their children speaks volumes of the class hierarchies that shape student mobility out of South Korea.

For Seunghui, the choice to enter UIC was a de facto option when her plans to attend college in the United States disappeared in the aftermath of the global financial crisis. Like many South Korean students who are groomed within elite educational tracks, Seunghui learned within an exacting curriculum designed to fit the entry requirements of a college choice that had already been made before she even began high school. But when life circumstances unexpectedly changed her plans, the decision she and her parents had made no longer served its original purpose. The opportunity to study at UIC still allowed her to attend a prestigious university and benefit from her global cultural capital without having to pay the high price of American tuition. Yet the fact that even someone as advantaged as Seunghui still faced uncertainties in her college admissions prospects underscores the pervasive fragility that even the most well-prepared students can experience, in South Korea and beyond.[21]

For Taeho, the choice to attend Santa Monica College and, ultimately, UC Berkeley was an escape from his lack of choices within South Korea. He was a first-generation college student who never had the advantages of early study abroad or other forms of extramural learning, and the chances of his attaining educational success in South Korea were slim. Each choice he made set him on a rewarding path but was also tempered by the setbacks that he faced, whether it was failing the college entrance exam, struggling through English proficiency requirements, navigating unfamiliar campus expectations, or paying his own tuition and living expenses by working illegally at restaurants in California. His admirable determination to succeed against all odds makes him an anomaly among the students whom I met. Taeho also challenges the stereotype that study abroad is a privileged choice for privileged individuals.

For Brandon, enrolling at UIC was really the only choice he had if he wanted to pursue a college education. Fluent in English but with no citizenship status in the United States, he also lacked the Korean fluency necessary to allow him entry into a South Korean university. An international college taught entirely in English was his only option in South Korea, especially as his questionable residency status in the United States precluded his opportunities to attend college there. Brandon was indeed internationally mobile, but his mobility was anything but flexible. His transnational trajectory was not so much an exercise of flexible citizenship but instead beholden to the configurations of his actual citizenship, which in South Korea demand cultural and linguistic fluency for full participation and military service needs that he had yet to meet for full recognition.[22]

How much choice did these students really have? The experiences of these four individuals certainly raise important questions of agency for South Korean students.[23] As we have seen, their choices were shaped by the structural realities that they faced alongside the opportunities afforded to them by the schools they ended up attending. Universities nonetheless label such students as flexible citizens, a term that I hope to have shown is in tension with their actual experiences. Working from the assumption that they must compete for these internationally mobile students, universities repurpose their existing mechanisms into new arrangements that cater to students' needs. They do this by facilitating alternative admissions pathways. Ironically, the very creation of these pathways reflects how universities are able to make possible students' "choices" in the first place. In other words, the availability of students' choices ultimately reflects the flexibility of the universities rather than the students.

Summary

International student mobility is not solely an individual pursuit but is inextricably linked with universities' financial opportunities and constraints. In South Korea, against a rigid college admissions system that demands careful planning and extensive family resources, some students make a choice to pursue an alternative pathway into a selective university in Berkeley or Seoul. But such a choice to go abroad or stay at home does not necessarily render them flexible citizens but rather reflects the limited range of choices each student faced as they weighed their present realities and future opportunities. Meanwhile, their choices were only possible because universities in Berkeley and Seoul created these pathways in the first place.

Four students—Jihun, Seunghui, Taeho, and Brandon—made such a choice to exit, or otherwise bypass, the rigid college admissions system in South Korea. For Jihun and Seunghui, their experience is representative of the choice that many other South Korean students made as they enrolled at a community college in California or an international college in South Korea. Both already possessed English fluency gained during early study abroad experiences, which undoubtedly helped them enter. Yet their tenuous circumstances show how even well-positioned students can be equally pushed out of the hypercompetitive college admissions tracks in South Korea just as much as they chose to pursue alternative pathways into selective universities. But in the case of Taeho and Brandon, their experience is an extreme example that leaves some students with few, if any, options. The choice to enroll at a community college in California or an international college in South Korea were really their only options as they were blocked from pursuing other avenues. Yet they still faced assumptions of class privilege because of their international mobility, even as their actual experiences deviated quite dramatically. Ultimately, the trajectories of these four students that cut across Berkeley and Seoul upend the image of the flexible citizen as uninhibited globetrotters with an unlimited array of choices.

5

The Global Student Supply Chain

Right before the COVID-19 pandemic halted international student mobility in 2020, I gave a talk at an organization called Graduate School USA in Washington, DC. Despite its name, Graduate School USA is not a graduate school but a workforce training center for federal employees, with an unofficial motto that reads "where the government goes for government training." The institution began under the auspices of the Department of Agriculture in 1921 and branched off as an independent organization ninety years later. Yet it still operates mostly with federal funding and grants, one of which commissioned my talk.

By this time, I was no longer a student nor a staff member but a professor at Georgetown University, and such speaking invitations had begun to come my way more regularly. At Graduate School USA, my role was to address the challenges that international students face when applying to college in the United States. My audience was a group of high school guidance counselors, each one from a different foreign language high school in South Korea. A few had once been international students in the United States, while others had limited personal experience of study abroad. They were all part of a US tour organized by Graduate School USA to learn more about American higher education so that they could better advise their students. Their visit was funded by a State Department grant designed to increase the number of students coming from South Korea to the United States. These guidance counselors were accompanied by quite the entourage: Graduate School USA employees, U.S. Embassy officers from Seoul, academics from local universities, and interpreters for hire. After I gave my talk and answered questions, the motley crew embarked on a cross-country tour to visit American campuses and professional associations.

The convergence of these eclectic individuals—myself included—from across the education and quasi-education, public and private, and profit and nonprofit sectors spanning the United States and South Korea was a perfect microcosm of the diverse stakeholders who play a part in international student mobility. Each stakeholder fulfills particular objectives that shape the pathways that students take and the choices that students make. Yet attention is usually placed upon solely the universities or the students. Even the previous chapters of this book focus on how universities create the pathways that allow students to be internationally mobile and how students choose to pursue them. The purpose of this chapter, however, is to identify the range of individual and institutional actors that broker the relationship between universities and students through intricate encounters and configurations.

In this chapter, I show how an expansive ecosystem of ancillary people and organizations funnel students to specific universities according to market demands and reinforce the global student supply chain between Berkeley and Seoul. I map out different parts of a larger industry of global higher education by examining the role of education agents, admissions recruiters, special purpose high schools, quasi-regulatory bodies, and governmental agencies. The industry expanded alongside universities' student recruitment efforts in the postrecession decade. I foreground each part of this dynamic industry with a structural analysis of its complex workings. I also contextualize these analyses with ethnographic vignettes of key industry insiders. These individuals negotiate larger industry pressures with their own motivations and goals that further capitalize on the global aspirations of South Korean students.

The Rise of Education Agents

In their seminal 2014 article in the *International Migration Review*, the anthropologists Biao Xiang and Johan Lindquist discuss the notion of migration infrastructure, which they define as "systematically interlinked technologies, institutions, and actors that facilitate and condition mobility."[1] Quoting Bruno Latour, they point out that it would be inaccurate to claim that an airplane flies; rather, the act of flying is part of an interconnected system of airports, launch pads, ticket counters, and so forth. By analogy, Xiang and Lindquist argue that migrants migrate not by their own agency but rather a broad expanse of human and nonhuman actors that mediate the process of migration. Since the publication of their work, numerous empirical studies have grafted the concept of migration infrastructure onto various migration industries to explore how infrastructures might advance or constrain migration.[2]

When examining migration infrastructure within Asia, scholars have advanced the concept of brokerage to describe the remarkable growth of governmental organizations, private companies, international groups, employment agencies, and educational institutions that facilitate and condition the movement of people.[3] As Tina Shrestha and Brenda Yeoh note, the practice of brokerage unfolds through unpredictable encounters and misinterpretations. This makes the practice of brokerage, as well as those classified as brokers, susceptible to charges of moral ambiguity, and even dubiousness, within this "black box of migration."[4]

At the heart of the "black box" of international student mobility is the education agent. Education agents recruit international students to colleges and universities on a commission basis, even though they are not actually employed by the schools for which they recruit. They typically operate through international recruitment agencies, which enter into contracts with colleges and universities that award a percentage of first-year tuition for each student who enrolls through an agent's efforts, typically in the range of 10 to 15 percent.[5] These for-profit agencies can also contract with multiple schools simultaneously without much oversight around conflicts of interest. This incentive structure has raised alarm across the higher education sector, with critics arguing that education agents, and the agencies where they work, do not represent students' best interests.

Whether desirable or not, the reality is that education agents are now firmly part of the global higher education landscape. There are estimates of over twenty thousand international recruitment agencies operating worldwide, with differences across location, size, and recruitment specializations.[6] Partnering with agencies is common for higher education institutions in the United Kingdom and Australia, where they have had to take on more aggressive recruitment tactics because they are competing with the global dominance of higher education in the United States. But while this commercial partnership has historically been limited in the United States, more recently there has been a definitive shift. According to a joint survey conducted in 2021 by the National Association for College Admissions Counseling and the American International Recruitment Council, nearly half of colleges and universities surveyed indicated that they partner with agencies to recruit overseas undergraduate students—of which a third said that they had increased their number of partners since the start of the pandemic.[7]

The exact number of international recruitment agencies in South Korea, known locally as yuhagwon, is unclear, largely because the industry is unregulated. Estimates indicate around one thousand agencies, though fewer than one hundred agencies account for 90 percent of market share in South Korea.[8] The industry rapidly expanded in the late 1990s and 2000s alongside the liberalization of the education sector and the explosion of the shadow education market. Today, most agencies lump their services in bundles—for example, by providing education consulting alongside English language learning, test preparation, visa processing, or housing services— especially as they connect their services to other service providers within South Korea and the host countries where students study.[9] The majority operate as small businesses concentrated in the Gangnam area of Seoul run by individuals who rely on word-of-mouth referrals and who frequently go in and out of business with the changing tides of South Korea's economy.

Though the industry itself is unregulated, there are a number of professional associations through which education agents can connect with one another. The largest and most prominent is called the Korea Overseas Study Association (KOSA). The association was founded in 1987 by a small group of education agents and other industry professionals. In the early years of the organization's establishment and growth, this close network of individuals created a forum through which they could share information and help newcomers establish their business, which certainly helped propel the study abroad industry in South Korea. Today, its primary activities involve ensuring that its member agents follow its code of ethics while connecting them with referral requests that come through the U.S. and British Embassies. The organization has grown and evolved over the decades, but recently membership has waned as the study abroad industry has become much less centralized and education agents have become much less dependent on a single referral channel.

The waxing and waning of such activities are a hallmark of this dynamic industry in South Korea. In fact, education agents are seasoned veterans when it comes to weathering disruption, whether it was the Asian financial crisis of the late 1990s or the global financial crisis of the late 2000s. The onset of the COVID-19 pandemic and the abrupt halt in overseas travel has certainly presented another major challenge for those who work in this industry. Even so, the industry itself will certainly survive under new circumstances and evolving demands.

Working as an Education Agent

It all started with her children. After Hyeonsuk sent her son and daughter to highly selective boarding schools and then highly selective universities, both in the United States, other South Korean parents began asking her for help doing the same for their children. At the time, she was working as an English teacher at a hagwon, where she taught extramural classes to children of affluent parents from Gangnam. For five years, Hyeonsuk helped these parents free of charge until she launched her own consulting business in 1994. By then, she had amassed a network of parents with high hopes and global aspirations for their children. Even today, her clients are secured exclusively through word-of-mouth referrals.

Hyeonsuk has garnered a reputation as one of the premier education agents in South Korea. Her high level of professionalism has made her a standard bearer for the industry, and her popular guidebook to studying abroad solidified her reputation among parents. Her children, now adults, finished their education abroad and returned to South Korea. In their late thirties and early forties, her son works as a diplomatic officer and her daughter works in a private company. Meanwhile, Hyeonsuk stays active across different areas of the study abroad industry in South Korea. Her bread and butter, though, is her consulting business, through which she provides tailored advice to South Koreans who want to study in the United States. She doesn't contract with specific schools. Rather, she provides a high-touch experience for a rarefied class of students and parents able and willing to pay for her services and who want what she calls "real advice" that will ultimately gain them entry into highly selective universities. Her services are provided over a long duration of time, with parents seeking her out as early as when their children are in the sixth grade.

But Hyeonsuk is pragmatic. Having worked in the industry for a long time, she has witnessed firsthand the shrinking number of South Korean students going abroad since the Great Recession and is acutely aware that business comes and goes. So she has her hand in several different pots. She works as a consultant for an international secondary school in Songdo. She also works as a staff member at an international recruitment agency in Gangnam, where she also provides admissions advice to US-bound students. Meanwhile, that agency sets up contracts with several overseas schools.

Most agencies in South Korea offer both customer-facing and business-facing services. Customer-facing services are what are offered to students and parents as they seek out the advice of education agents in preparation for their study abroad endeavors. This particular agency aggressively markets and sells services such as admissions advice, essay consulting, test preparation, private tutoring, GPA management, extracurricular interest planning, parent-teacher relationship management—the list goes on. These services are provided by a team of staff members, including Hyeonsuk, who each possess distinct specializations (e.g., STEM fields, art and music, pre-law, premedicine) and whose own educational credentials are prominently displayed on the agency's marketing materials. Business-facing services are the recruitment activities that are offered to overseas schools. This particular agency enters into contracts with overseas colleges and universities, as well as private high schools, that want to grow their student numbers from South Korea. The terms of each contract vary depending on each school's enrollment goals, but the agency typically charges an upfront fee in exchange for sending a minimum number of students over a certain period of time.

While the customer-facing services that Hyeonsuk offers through her staff position at the agency and through her individual consulting business may look similar, she operates with subtly different ethical standards. On the one hand, the services she offers at the more mass-market agency may be more customer pleasing but are also more contractual. Hyeonsuk has a negative view of some of her mass-market clients, as she explained to me,

> [The students] want to save their time. Because if someone wants to apply to Georgetown, for example, I can say they are lazy. They should do their own personal essay, but they don't. They want to save their time. They give some money. Got it from parents. Give it to yuhagwon. They are lazy. Even though I help them, I think they are lazy. (laughs)

On the other hand, the services she offers through her individual consulting business are more demanding of her clients with an understanding of longer-term outcomes.

> Real one, they have their own [essay]. But still, they want some help. For example, like essay, they should write their own. However, they sometimes ask for help. Just correct some grammar is okay. But sometimes I say, "I can't help you on this one. You should find your own idea. That point I cannot help." Then they try for another yuhagwon. My main philosophy is honesty and trust. Honesty is most important. And finally, when they do spend their own time writing their essay, then they say, "Thank you for your advice. I can find my own way. I passed. I got acceptance."

Now in her sixties, Hyeonsuk is a seasoned veteran who spent decades cultivating a community of professionals who also hold high ethical standards in the study abroad industry. And like many individuals of a certain age, she grouses about the younger generation of education agents, who she says only cares about making money and running a successful business. In our conversations, she contrasted the more mass-market agency's heavy-handed services and contractual arrangements with the higher standards and individualized attention of her consulting business. But as agencies adopt a customer-comes-first approach and hustle for more school contracts, the reality is that education agents like Hyeonsuk still work fluidly across such evolving contexts, even if primarily for their own survival within a highly commercialized industry.

When we connected over Zoom (because the pandemic prevented me from traveling to Seoul), Hyeonsuk talked about the many colleagues who had gone out of business as the COVID-19 pandemic upended the industry. None of this is new for her. She has already seen declining numbers of South Korean students going overseas as the country's youth unemployment rate balloons and an overseas degree becomes less advantageous in the South Korean job market. In the last five to ten years, she has seen more South Korean students opt for international schools in South Korea, or even neighboring China, due to their physical proximity and relatively lower cost. The COVID-19 pandemic has only exacerbated this because parents are worried about sending their children very far from home. New business is slow for Hyeonsuk, too, and she decided now was a good time to prepare for retirement. As she was winding down her professional activities, she still regularly met with her long-time colleagues, those whom she called "almost retired" like herself, to share meals and talk shop. But as long as South Koreans want to study abroad, Hyeonsuk told me, they will continue to seek out her services.

> I cannot quit my job because even the few people, they want me to help them still. That's why even if it's slow, I couldn't quit . . . We cannot imagine what will happen in the future. But one important thing is, America is always the first destination for Korean people.

By the end of our conversation, the topic focused less on her work and more on mine. Hyeonsuk, an entrepreneur, saw a business opportunity. How many South Korean students are enrolled at my university? What about the program that I direct? Am I looking to increase international enrollments? Hyeonsuk was particularly interested in my program's online offerings and offered to connect me with the international recruitment agency where she works as a staff member. Like I said, the industry itself is poised to thrive under new circumstances and evolving demands.

Community College International Recruitment Strategies

If an international recruitment agency's currency is its local net-works, then a higher education institution's currency is its global positioning. But this is precisely what some schools lack as they enter the global student marketplace. "We're not UC Berkeley," said one senior international officer of a California community college. Indeed, UC Berkeley has an explicit policy of not partnering with agencies.[10] But many of California's community colleges have no such policy and do indeed partner with them.

What makes these partnerships valuable for community colleges is the assumption that agencies possess more and better information than the college does. Using "agency theory" to explain the relation-ship between higher education institutions and international recruit-ment agencies, the higher education scholars Pii-Tuulia Nikula and Jussi Kivistö outline the reasons why a school would want to partner with one.[11] The appeal of agencies is that they are more familiar with local market conditions and cultures, can verify documents submit-ted by students, and provide local networks that the school may lack. They also provide a cost-effective alternative to maintaining a continuous presence around the globe without having to set up offices or send employees to travel.

Some community colleges have partnered with agencies for many years already. Their long-standing relationships with international recruitment agencies go hand-in-hand with their reputation as feeder schools into the UC campuses, a reputation that is promoted by the community colleges themselves and then marketed by the agencies with which they partner. As I discussed in chapter 2, places like De Anza College and Diablo Valley College have a reputation among international students as pathways into UC Berkeley. Those schools send large numbers of international students as transfer students to UC Berkeley each year. For the last decade, international students have constituted a third—and in some years nearly half—of the total number of De Anza and Diablo Valley transfer students to UC Berkeley each year. Both community colleges also have a long history of partnering with agencies for nearly two decades, and most of those agencies are based in Asia. In recent years, many California community colleges have scaled up their international recruitment efforts from the college level to the district level. This means that agency partnerships for De Anza and Diablo Valley are now managed across the Foothill-De Anza and Contra Costa Community College Districts, respectively.

What struck me when speaking to the individuals who oversee international recruitment across community college districts was that the activities they undertake are at once mercenary and mundane. They talked at length about the strategies they undertake to make the community colleges within their district more competitive than the community colleges outside it, even though they recognized that they are all part of the same system. In their book *Broke*, published in 2021, sociologists Laura Hamilton and Kelly Nielsen point out how higher education leaders can view other institutions within the same system as competitors under conditions of austerity.[12] International recruitment leaders for community college districts with whom I spoke frequently referenced community colleges in neighboring districts as their primary competitors, which then affected how they strategized their agency contracts with more attractive commission rates so that agencies would funnel more students to them rather than their competitors. Meanwhile, they also described the humdrum administrative tasks that propel this rivalry, such as standardizing contract terms, synchronizing payment of commission fees, working creatively within shrinking budgets, and managing a team of admissions recruiters.

In fact, a number of individuals noted that an essential part of international recruitment involves not just overseeing a portfolio of agency partnerships but also employing a team of admissions recruiters, who serve as the primary points of contact for the agencies with which the districts partner. For instance, both districts of Foothill-De Anza and Contra Costa employ recruiters who are responsible for and physically based in key regions of the districts' international recruitment strategy, especially in Asia, the region where they partner with the greatest number of agencies. In addition to sustaining and growing agency partnerships, recruiters monitor local conditions in the sending countries where they recruit and provide valuable information back to the district offices. And like their agent counterparts, recruiters are themselves paid on a contract basis on terms that are as flexible as month to month, especially as budget constraints have limited the spending power of the districts to hire recruiters on a full-time basis.

As the COVID-19 pandemic further shrinks revenue streams, district offices are working with even smaller budgets while competition for international students becomes fiercer. Recently, community colleges in neighboring states like Washington have started to compete with California community colleges for international students. Additionally, the rise of pathway providers within the last decade, such as Shorelight and INTO, introduces a new set of challenges, as these behemoth corporations are able to offer commission rates that are five to ten times higher than what California community colleges offer. Amid these trying times, California community colleges continue to emphasize their high transfer rates to selective UC schools even more vehemently while under steady pressure to find new competitive advantages.

Working as a Community College Admissions Recruiter

It's a beautiful autumn morning in the San Francisco Bay Area, but this admissions recruiter would never know it, sitting in his office halfway around the world. John works as an admissions recruiter for a California community college district well known for its feeder school into UC Berkeley, but he lives in and spends the better part of his time recruiting throughout Asia, a region of great importance to the district where he is employed. On this particular morning, he sat down to chat with me after eating his breakfast. Meanwhile, I was up late at night in my home in the Washington, DC metropolitan area. Each of us sat on opposite ends of the world nowhere near California yet were tethered by a Zoom meeting.

Though based in another part of Asia, John travels to South Korea regularly to recruit students for the California community college district as well as a for-profit business school in New York. Both of these employ him on a contract basis; at least they did until the latter contract ended when the pandemic began. He assured me that this was not a conflict of interest because the schools don't compete for the same kind of students. His personal code of ethics is such that he would never recruit simultaneously on behalf of schools that do compete, though he mentioned skeptically that many other recruiters do. He holds a matter-of-fact view about his work. "Either you're out there recruiting, or you've got the name that pulls them in," he told me plainly.

When John was a student, he attended universities with "the name to pull them in." A graduate of Harvard and Oxford, he studied history and theology before working in staff positions in international education offices at US universities. In the 1990s he segued into international marketing and recruitment roles for for-profit education management companies, positions that took him all over the world. Now, he prefers working as a consultant, juggling multiple contracts for schools that seek out his marketing and recruitment acumen. And over the years, he has worked for UC Extension schools and Cal State universities, as well as competitor community college districts.

John and the many admissions recruiters like him sit at a notable point along the global student supply chain. As an admissions recruiter, he is officially recognized as a representative for whichever school that hires him. As a contract employee, he also has the latitude to represent multiple schools simultaneously, which creates ambiguities around where one school's recruitment activities begin and another's ends. Admissions recruiters such as John are also literal extensions of the increasingly global recruitment strategies of the schools that hire them. Ironically, it is the very schools that are the last to be recognized as global that adopt such aggressively global tactics, exactly because they lack the global positioning.

For the California community college district where John recruits, South Korea has been on their radar for quite some time, and his recruitment trips there have become fairly routine. His visits usually coincide with an education fair or tour, such as those hosted by EducationUSA or Linden Tours, so that he can meet with prospective students and parents, visit high schools, and connect with his vast file of agents. His extensive network of agents across Asia makes him an attractive admissions recruiter to US colleges and universities, he told me. He amassed his contacts over the decades that he had worked across the nonprofit and for-profit education sectors, marketing and recruiting on behalf of schools and companies. He recognized that working with agents is a contentious part of the admissions process, but he noted that the community colleges across California all seem comfortable with using them. He did acknowledge, however, that the practice has become much more ubiquitous in recent years and therefore much less controversial.

When he travels to South Korea, his work with agencies entails providing them with the most up-to-date admissions policies and practices of the schools that he represents, training their new staff members so that they can provide the right messaging to prospective students, and establishing an open line of communication that continues beyond his trips. The benefit of working with agencies, according to him, is that they tailor their advice to students and parents in service of the small selection of schools with which they partner. The tailored advice that students and parents would get is that attending a community college opens up a more accessible path to UC Berkeley. He told me,

> We know we are easier to get into. No community college should pretend that it's difficult to enter. The national, political, social, educational philosophy of community college is ease of entry. The irony of it is: we give you the best access to top universities, and when you graduate, you are getting the degree from the next university. I tell them, we can be your secret. (laughs) You don't have to tell anybody you went to a community college. We know what we do is great. And we know what we can do can help you move onto an elite school, *if* you do the work and *if* you have the smarts. And I have told parents straight out, look, if your kid is dumb and lazy, they're not going to go to UC Berkeley. (laughs)

By contrast, working with governmental agencies such as Education-USA means that those advising offices equally represent all four thousand higher education institutions in the United States and therefore cannot possibly provide effective advice to prospective students.

John's work in South Korea spans decades, and this has provided him with a unique perspective. He shared his observations on how South Korean students used to begin their overseas studies through intensive English programs in the United States and that he had recruited heavily for those programs in years past. He noted that intensive English programs were the original admissions pipelines into US colleges and universities for South Korean students who sought entry by unconventional means, along with boarding schools in the United States, long before community colleges became another one.[13] He has also observed the ebbs and flows of outbound student mobility across Asia over two financial crises, and likely now a third amid a pandemic.

Aside from broader macroeconomic forces, the factors that most affect his work in South Korea today are negative perceptions of community colleges and shrinking demographics. But negative perceptions of community colleges have certainly waned among students and parents and are primarily a leftover idea held fastidiously by high school representatives who just want to boast of the elite placements of their graduates. By contrast, shrinking demographics have led to increasing competition not just internationally but also domestically. He told me,

> On one of my trips within the last two or three years, meeting with one of our Korean agents for twenty years, he looked at me, he said, "The Korean universities are desperate to attract students. They will do anything. They're competing directly with you." That meant community colleges. That meant four-year schools. So that in protection of their own self-interest, the Korean universities have become much more aggressive in recruiting their own.

In fact, such increasing competition comes not just from universities but also from other institutional actors that operate in tandem with them.

Foreign Language High School Sending Strategies

세계로 뻗는 품격높은 한국인이 된다! *Koreans branching around the world!* It's a fitting motto for Daewon Foreign Language High School, the most renowned foreign language high school in South Korea. The school is famous for its global leadership program, which prepares students to study abroad at US colleges and universities. For a time in the late 2000s, when the number of South Korean students enrolled across US colleges and universities peaked at over seventy-five thousand, American publications such as *The New York Times*, *The Wall Street Journal*, and *Newsweek* ran pieces that marveled at Daewon's demanding curriculum and successful placement rates into Ivy League schools.[14] What began in the early 1990s under the South Korean government's efforts to globalize the country led to the burgeoning of these foreign language high schools, where the oft-stated goal is to cultivate students' foreign language capabilities and mold them into citizens of the world.[15] As of 2021 there were thirty of these special purpose high schools, all of which enjoy a high level of autonomy within the South Korean education system.[16]

While these high schools constitute a tiny proportion of the secondary education sector, they have an outsize influence in college admissions. Among the different kinds of special purpose high schools, foreign language high schools in particular have developed a reputation as college preparatory programs for students who can afford to attend. Students select a specific track upon entry that prepares them for the admissions requirements of selective universities, in South Korea or overseas. The domestic track focuses on cultivation of a foreign language in addition to English (usually Chinese, French, German, Japanese, or Spanish) to prepare students for the special admissions requirements of South Korean universities, as discussed in chapter 4. The international track provides an English immersion coupled with SAT preparation and Advanced Placement coursework to prepare students for study in the United States. Both tracks supplement their rigorous academic curriculum with an intense program of extracurricular activities.

Foreign language high schools also serve as domestic extensions of South Korean students' early study abroad endeavors. In the mid-1990s, a growing number of South Korean students enrolled in high schools in the United States as a prelude to their entry into US colleges and universities. South Korean media initially celebrated the practice as a transformative learning experience, but public opinion soon changed, as parents came to chastise study abroad in high school as a source of teenage corruption that turned students into feckless young adults corrupted by American consumerism and individualism.[17] Eventually, such discourses settled on something more moderated by advancing the notion of the "right" kind of study abroad: one or two years of early study abroad during a child's elementary school years, followed by enrollment in a foreign language high school in South Korea, and then matriculation at a US college or university.[18] Such understanding of the appropriate timing and duration of study abroad further fueled the popularity of foreign language high schools as a critical stepping stone in between early study abroad and college.

In short, foreign language high schools have become early tracking mechanisms that further stratify the haves and have-nots in South Korea, which is exactly why they are now in danger of losing their special status.[19] Alongside recent policy initiatives to reduce the proportion of students that universities are allowed to admit through special admissions, the South Korean government has also vowed to take away the autonomy of foreign language high schools, which enables them to set their own admissions requirements and offer a specialized curriculum exempt from national policies. These legislative efforts have struck a nerve for many, with parents taking to the streets to protest. These proposed changes, as well as the backlash against them, reflect a deep status anxiety on the part of those who benefit from a stratified school system in South Korea.

Meanwhile, foreign language high schools have begun to reshape their curricula to better meet the needs of today's students, who are increasingly looking to their higher education options within South Korea. In fact, a representative of Daewon Foreign Language High School told me that only 10 out of 260 students from the graduating class of 2021 opted to go abroad, which prompted conversations about whether to even continue their renowned global leadership program. And as the admissions process into selective universities in South Korea becomes more competitive, foreign language high schools are encouraging students who study in the domestic track to supplement their education with SAT preparation and Advanced Placement coursework normally reserved for those in the international track so as to give them an extra boost amid ever-evolving admissions requirements.

Indeed, the strict separation between the domestic and international tracks no longer makes as much sense as it did when originally established, especially as newer varieties of special admissions have emerged in South Korea. For example, international colleges in South Korea follow neither special nor regular admissions. Instead, they require something more akin to the admissions requirements of a US college or university, as discussed in chapter 3. As a result, many foreign language high schools have launched a specialized sub-track designed for students who want to prepare specifically for the admissions requirements of international colleges in South Korea. This makes domestic students' arrival into places like Yonsei's Underwood International College less an accident and more like any other admissions track into a selective university in South Korea. And as the admissions requirements of selective universities continue to evolve, so, too, do the curricular offerings of foreign language high schools that carefully align the preparation of their students for even newer entryways.

Working as a Foreign Language High School Teacher

Gayeong has been a teacher at a foreign language high school in Seoul for nearly two decades. After completing her master's degree in TESOL at Arizona State University, she was hired as an English teacher for the high school's international track. She herself attended a similar high school, as had her younger sister, which was the main reason she wanted to work there. Today, her seniority and experience have made her a homeroom teacher, a position that requires her to wear many hats as a teacher, guidance counselor, and program administrator for the high school's international track. She described what she does as "life guidance," which covers everything from helping students in their course selection, tracking their grade point average, to chaperoning them during night study. "We are like parents at school," she said. Indeed, homeroom teachers spend a lot more time with students than their parents do and are often with them from 7:30 in the morning until 10:00 at night.

Being a homeroom teacher also means that Gayeong oversees students' college admissions endeavors. This is how we were first introduced, as she was one of the individuals selected to participate in the US tour for high school guidance counselors organized by Graduate School USA. Though there is an official guidance counselor at the high school where she works, it is the homeroom teacher who is expected to guide students and parents in the "big picture" strategizing of college admissions. But in this regard, Gayeong's role is one of formality rather than substance. Switching between English and Korean, she shared with me how she goes about admissions advising.

> I try not to go overboard, always, when giving advice to students. To my gut feeling, students and parents, they already know what they want and what to do. So they are not really asking for advice—*from me*. They have everything they need from outside source. And even if they are asking me like they're asking for advice, it's like 20 percent of counseling cases. It's more like they want to get approval. [Can I say this in Korean? From my point of view, they already come to me like they have a plan and just ask me to check it at the very end. Just check it at the very end. Those who actually need information from me only amount to 10 or 20 percent. Other people, when they come to me], they have money, they have information. The parents are very intelligent and the elite of our society. They know all the information. They have money, they know where to go, where to pull strings. [So when they come to me for guidance, they just say to me, "Teacher, this is what we are going to do. What do you think?" That's how I feel.]

Gayeong went on to describe how a small selection of education agencies in a very exclusive neighborhood of Gangnam, called Daechi-dong, are where students and parents acquire the college admissions advice that they do not need from her. Rather than the mass-market agencies that go for bulk, these specialized agencies cater exclusively to students at foreign language high schools. For Gayeong, this is actually a positive development.

> Can I be really frank? We have so much work to do. We work more than other high school or middle school teachers, but we are paid pretty much the same. So it's like they are reducing the workload. I feel like that way. It's like we are living together. Gongsaeng hada [symbiotic]. We help each other. Win-Win. Even if I study abroad for my master's degree, I wasn't trained as a guidance counselor for high school students. I never had a chance to send high school students to overseas colleges. If I want to be really professional, I have to spend extra time in that process, but then I have to sacrifice my family and sometimes even my health. So I can't help it.

The high school benefits, too, if the end result is that students are accepted into a selective university, which enhances the high school's reputation. As Gayeong succinctly put it, "We educate here, and they give information there."

As a homeroom teacher for the international track, she also engages in administrative activities related to international education. She connects students with admissions recruiters from overseas colleges and universities who are invited to visit the high school. She rattled off some familiar names among US schools, all of them highly selective, that send representatives and hold information sessions. But over the last decade, she has watched the number of students who want to study abroad drastically shrink, and this has affected her work in notable ways. Her high school no longer seeks new relationships with overseas school representatives. The number of teachers hired in the international track has shrunk by a third. And the official guidance counselor's position has converted into a part-time affiliate position. From her perspective, parents don't see a compelling reason to send their children to the United States unless they are admitted to HYPS, an acronym they use to refer to Harvard, Yale, Princeton, and Stanford. Parents are more likely to trust the quality of education offered at South Korean universities, she told me. They regard studying abroad as one option among many and no longer the status symbol that it once was.

Indeed, Gayeong's job gives her firsthand knowledge of the latest college sending strategies. One increasingly popular strategy, she told me, is the special admissions track into South Korean universities for those classified as Overseas Koreans. It's the same track that international colleges offer to formally recognize the unique needs of transnational returnees, but more recently, a growing number of universities offer it among their suite of admissions tracks across all their departments to further encourage the repatriation of South Korean citizens living abroad. In tandem with this shift in the higher education sector, the South Korean government opened Korean International Schools, which follow the K–12 national curriculum but otherwise operate in other countries in order to prepare South Koreans living abroad for entry into South Korean universities.[20] Government efforts to repatriate their students who go abroad are what the scholars Rachel Brooks and Johanna Waters refer to as "an obstruction of overseas diaspora formation," in which the state intentionally creates pathways back to overseas students' home countries in order to capitalize on their human capital contributions.[21] But beyond serving as a pathway to repatriation for South Korean citizens living abroad, Korean International Schools have also become another admissions pipeline into South Korean universities for South Korean students within South Korea, who go abroad just to attend these schools and qualify as Overseas Koreans. Seen in this way, Korean International Schools have become direct competitors of foreign language high schools by taking advantage of an unusual admissions track that only students residing abroad can use.

In fact, this was the sending strategy that Gayeong was seriously considering for her son, who was finishing the eighth grade and about to enter high school. At the time we reconnected following her visit to Washington, DC, she was watching her son struggle with online learning during the pandemic and worrying about his college prospects as he fell behind in school. Though her job entails preparing highly competitive high school students for highly competitive college admissions tracks, she wasn't confident that her son would be successful in pursuing them himself. She contemplated sending him to a country in Southeast Asia, probably Vietnam or Thailand, so that he could attend a Korean International School there and qualify as an Overseas Korean, which would give him a leg up in the admissions process when returning to South Korea as a college student. She was also intrigued by the prospect of sending him to a community college in the United States so that he could transfer into a selective university there—an admissions pipeline she learned about while on the US tour with Graduate School USA. Ironically, she would never recommend these options for the students at the foreign language high school where she works. This time, however, she was navigating college sending strategies not for the benefit of her employer's reputation but her own son.

Establishing Ethical Standards in College Admissions

As high school guidance counselors have become increasingly involved in the college admissions process, they have also become influential members of professional organizations dedicated to this activity. The most prominent in the United States is the National Association of College Academic Counselors (NACAC), which was founded in 1937 and consists of over twenty-three thousand members from around the world, most of whom are high school guidance counselors or college admissions personnel. The association establishes ethical standards and best practices in college admissions and disseminates them through its Guide to Ethical Practice in College Admission, what its members regard as the most influential document of their profession.[22]

For many years, NACAC prohibited the use of incentive compensation for college admissions and used punitive measures against member institutions that were found to be in violation of its policy.

NACAC's policy actually mirrored US federal law prohibiting the same. Following federal investigations of exploitative student recruitment practices at vocational schools in the 1980s, Congress reauthorized the 1965 Higher Education Act in 1992 with new regulations.[23] A paragraph within Title IV stipulates that higher education institutions are not allowed to pay commission to third parties to recruit students who receive federal student aid. The intent was to prevent the for-profit higher education sector from preying on low-income students and profiting from US taxpayer money, a practice that the sociologist Tressie McMillan Cottom details in the 2017 book, *Lower Ed*.[24] However, Title IV of the reauthorized Higher Education Act also details an exception: that institutions could pay commission to third parties in order to recruit international students, who are not eligible for federal student aid.[25] This policy loophole effectively allows colleges and universities to employ education agents for international student recruitment even as they are prohibited from doing so for domestic student recruitment.

Even so, NACAC retained its own prohibitive policy until it was challenged during the "agent debates." These debates—what industry insiders call the period between 2011 and 2013 leading to NACAC's policy amendment—were a series of hearings held by a NACAC special commission to explore international student recruitment practices. Those in support of the use of agents in international student recruitment—mostly admissions professionals at schools that were already employing them—argued that the practice was already widespread and that NACAC urgently needed to create ethical guidelines around it. Meanwhile, critics who argued against the use of agents—mostly high school guidance counselors and other educators—pointed to the perverse incentives that authorizing for-profit international student recruitment practices would create. After two years of heated testimony and lots of headbutting, NACAC changed a single word in what was then called its Statement of Principles of Good Practice: that members "should not" provide incentive compensation for international student recruitment, changed from "may not." The association published its recommendations in a report that concluded the agent debates in 2013.[26]

Since those heady days of controversy, NACAC released updated versions of its influential document that use more inclusive language around incentive compensation. The association has also published extensive resources designed to guide its members who choose to work with agents. Moreover, a complex economy of quality assurance providers has emerged that work in tandem with NACAC's efforts. For instance, the American International Recruitment Council created a certification process based on US higher education accreditation practices to certify agencies that meet their quality assurance standards. The British Council also created a certification process to certify individual agents who undergo their training protocols. And across numerous sending countries of international students, professional associations for agents have emerged that serve as self-regulatory bodies, such as the Korea Overseas Study Association in South Korea. These country-specific associations are also often members of a global umbrella association called the Federation of Education and Language Consultant Associations (FELCA), a nonprofit association dedicated to ensuring quality services across agencies worldwide.

But even as NACAC officially greenlighted the practice of employing agents, the organization still navigates a murky ethical terrain. The US government effectively disallows the use of agents for domestic student recruitment while maintaining a policy loophole for international student recruitment. Professional associations may emphasize accountability, transparency, and integrity when using agents, but lingering notions of illegitimacy remain across the higher education sector because of NACAC's prior policy stance on incentive compensation. These circumstances lead to mixed messaging on the legitimacy of agents.

Working within a Quasi-regulatory Body

Rob vividly remembers the agent debates. At the time, he was working in the international admissions division at a California community college, where he was busy implementing a new recruitment model that made extensive use of agency partnerships. "To this day, I can take credit—or blame—for having brought that agent model," he told me half-jokingly. He became familiar with the world of agents when he recruited international students for the intensive English program of a Cal State university in the early 2000s, before bringing this institutional knowledge with him to the California community college. A Californian by upbringing, he entered this line of work after beginning his career as an English teacher in Japan and then transitioning into international education when moving back to California.

Rob's career took an interesting turn when he joined NACAC soon after the agent debates concluded. NACAC was faced with the task of putting in place its newly revised policy authorizing the use of agents. Rob's was a new role created to do just that. He moved from California to Arlington, Virginia, the location of NACAC's headquarters, to incorporate the organization's recommendation on agents into its various activities. He described his job at NACAC as one of great responsibility to the diverse stakeholders involved.

> I don't want to dwell too much on my individual experience, but having been there at the association during that peak of the controversy, the decision-making, and the change in the regulations, it was really, quite frankly, formative for me in terms of, wow, now I really understand the pros and the cons, the advocates and the detractors, where they're coming from. Because that code of practice was changed, the association, and myself included, felt pretty duty-bound to say, if we're going to "permit" this among our members, then we better start producing some best practice materials to help mitigate the risk. Not just to institutions and agents, primarily, but to students, because there's lots of risk.

Rob has authored much of NACAC's best practices materials. He and his colleagues have worked hard to normalize working with agents and make the intricacies of the practice less opaque. Still, he acknowledged that there is widespread reluctance across his profession to work with agents. He told me,

> There is still a good bit of trepidation on a lot of folks' parts who work in this space and are starting to consider working with agents. You even hear stories of, "Hey my VP or whoever wants us to start working with agents, but I don't know anything, and I don't know if we should." You also hear the opposite, where this person at this level wants to work with agents, but the VP is like, "Isn't that illegal?" So there's a lot of that going on, still.

Part of the skepticism, Rob concluded, is because best practices are difficult to enforce. He gave the example of NACAC's recommendation that colleges and universities clearly list all the agencies with which they partner on their website, a best practice that was formulated during his time there. Later, NACAC conducted a survey of colleges and universities inquiring whether this best practice was being followed, and the results showed that only a quarter of respondents were actually doing so. Transparency is at the core of NACAC's ethics, but it is difficult to enforce, Rob told me, because of the mixed messaging that comes directly from the US government.

> If you've got an activity that is essentially illegal in the United States context, it doesn't exactly pave the way to being very open and transparent about it internationally, notwithstanding good work of NACAC and other groups that have done best practice development and promotion.

Rob has since left NACAC and moved back into international student recruitment. His time there certainly left a mark on his professional development. He is active in public debates on the role of agents and has become a well-known scholar-practitioner in this area. In the numerous talks he gives as a scholar, he often argues for the need for better regulatory measures around agents. Speaking to me as a practitioner, however, he shared with me how he is skeptical of the efficacy of current regulatory measures. He explained how he regards the certificates issued by the American International Recruitment Council or British Council with a grain of salt. They may provide value to those who are just entering the global student marketplace and have less experience working with agents. For him, though, he gives greater weight to a colleague's attestations about working with a particular agent than a certificate. He understands that the industry is heavily relationship based, and he places a lot more emphasis on his social capital.

Rob brings a unique perspective. As someone who has worked within and beyond the regulatory environment, he sheds light on how NACAC and similar associations play an ambiguous role, serving as a regulator for international student recruitment but also having no enforcement capability. The ambiguity became even more pronounced when, in 2020, NACAC recast its influential document as an ethical guide rather than a mandatory code that its members must follow, due to pressure from an antitrust lawsuit by the Department of Justice.[27] Ultimately, Rob saw this as a smart move by NACAC, though one in which their hand was forced. He told me,

> The fact is, they weren't being followed, which is partly why the conversation ensued. Because there became this unavoidable pressure to say, "Well, it seems like we say no, you can't do this," and yet here is this growing subset of members that are actively doing it. What's up? We've got to reconcile that. So that gave rise to this process, and then they updated the language. I think it's followed in spirit, but I have to be honest, I've lost some touch with what's the latest SPGP, Statement of Principles of Good Practice. They've deliberately, probably smartly, loosened some of the language and made it less prescriptive and more general rules of thumb, in part because of the enforceability challenges.

The ambiguous role of quasi-regulatory bodies raises important questions as to which organization, ultimately, does regulate international student recruitment.

The Role of the US Government

When most of the world went into lockdown in early 2020, I learned of a new series of virtual talks hosted by the U.S. Commercial Service. Each talk focused on a specific country's student market and was intended for US-based higher education professionals interested in recruiting there. For the talk on South Korea, representatives from the Commercial Service's office in Seoul, who are also diplomatic officers of the U.S. Embassy, shared tips on how universities can continue to attract South Korean students amid the COVID-19 pandemic. At the end of the talk, they offered to connect those of us attending with education agents in South Korea personally vetted by their office. This new series of virtual talks were in line with the Commercial Service's broader mission to advance American commercial interests around the world. As the trade promotion arm of the Department of Commerce, the federal agency matches US-based companies with overseas agents, distributors, partners, and other local entities for a nominal fee. From this federal agency's perspective, universities are US-based companies, and education is highly regarded as the United States's sixth largest service export.

At the same time I was attending the talks, the Trump administration announced aggressive executive orders and proclamations targeting international students. Customs and Border Control prevented students from entering the United States, and Immigration and Customs Enforcement threatened deportation for students already in the United States. Indeed, as one federal agency followed directives to maintain or increase the number of international students, another followed entirely different directives to reduce their numbers or eliminate them entirely. The virtual talks hosted by the Commercial Service amid the Trump administration's efforts to block or remove international students were but one example of this disconnection. And this uncoordinated effort at the highest level of government in the United States reflects the lack of a clear national strategy around international student recruitment.

Divergent national strategies around international student recruitment arguably began when the 1965 Higher Education Act was reauthorized in 1992 and forbade higher education institutions from paying commission to third parties in student recruitment efforts, except in the case of international students, who are not eligible for federal student aid. In addition to establishing a policy loophole for education agents within international student recruitment, the reauthorized Higher Education Act effectively recognized international student recruitment as a commercial endeavor. This followed decades of a different US government strategy during the Cold War, when international student recruitment was recognized primarily as a diplomatic effort to "win hearts and minds."[28]

In most cases, the dual roles of international students, as commercial and diplomatic interests, have been beautifully aligned. But when the COVID-19 pandemic created unprecedented disruption and uncertainty, the US government ricocheted between two polar extremes, treating international students as financial assets to preserve or foreign invaders to fight off.[29] Nowhere was this policy divergence more evident than within the State Department, where the agency was ordered by the Trump administration to implement travel bans and visa restrictions on international students, while rank-and-file members continued to promote American interests abroad, including the promotion of American higher education overseas.

Indeed, the State Department is the federal agency that oversees international education and exchange, which makes international student recruitment a geopolitical project in the United States.[30] The State Department's Bureau of Educational and Cultural Affairs houses a number of offices that oversee international student recruitment, the most direct to do so being EducationUSA, which is the diplomatic arm through which the State Department promotes American higher education overseas. Its mission is to serve international students by providing reliable information about study opportunities in the United States and serve the American higher education community by assisting institutional leaders in meeting their recruitment goals. EducationUSA encompasses a vast network of 430 advising centers spanning 175 countries and territories. In South Korea, the advising center operates in close coordination with the U.S. Embassy in Seoul alongside other federal agencies such as the Commercial Service.

Notably, the EducationUSA advising center in South Korea has been aggressively promoting American higher education in order to reverse the trend of decreasing numbers of South Korean students headed to the United States. The center has launched several new campaigns, including one that promotes US community colleges to students outside of the Seoul metropolitan area. The diplomatic officers of the U.S. Embassy in Seoul seem to have made international student recruitment a priority, based on what they shared in our conversations, even as the political bombast coming from the United States sometimes sent a different message. These contradictions even within a single wing of the US government reflect how international student recruitment is hardly a cohesive endeavor at the highest level of authority in the United States.

Working as an EducationUSA Officer

I first came to know Jina when I was a Fulbright researcher in South Korea. We frequently crossed paths in the Fulbright Building in Seoul or at the events we both attended at the U.S. Embassy. Jina is part of the EducationUSA network, which makes her part of the US federal workforce, though she lives and works in Seoul. And as a federal worker, she is careful. Before we reconnected for an interview, she made clear to me that anything she said represented her personal views and not the views of EducationUSA or the US government.

Jina's job entails developing in-country projects for the EducationUSA advising center in South Korea. This includes organizing mentoring programs for South Korean students, setting up information sessions on behalf of US colleges and universities, and connecting South Korean students with representatives of US colleges and universities through education fairs. Her biggest priority, she told me, is to diversify the kinds of students who study in the United States. She talked at length about Seoul being an oversaturated market. Students outside of Seoul, however, remain overlooked and underprioritized. She told me,

> Personally, my priorities are just to highlight opportunity in general, but to get [higher education institutions] to think outside the box, because they tend to go where the numbers and the money are. Which is fine, because you have to follow the data, but it's reminding them that we create the data. The statistics are a momentary capture of what's happening, but some variable has to be influenced to make those statistics happen, right? I compare it to the iPhone. You don't need to sell the iPhone in a place where it's oversaturated and everybody has iPhones. It's like everyone in Seoul has the iPhone. Go a little bit outside of Seoul, and they're like, "I want the iPhone." Further outside of Seoul, it's like, "I don't think I can get the iPhone." And even further, "What's an iPhone?"

Her comments point to the immense influence of the global higher education industry—her office included—in shaping international student mobility flows. Jina believed her office to be an essential part of that.

One reason Seoul is such an oversaturated market, Jina told me, is because students there have easy access to information about studying abroad through a myriad of education agents. She described the immense pressure to employ the services of an agent, as well as the word-of-mouth method of finding one. Students seek out an agent because they believe everyone else is doing so, she told me, and they seek out the same agent that their classmates did, which further fuels the perception that doing so is universal. But lately, Jina has noticed that even students outside of Seoul are increasingly using agents. They rely on websites like Naver, a South Korean search engine that aggregates user-generated data, to find out which agents Seoul-based students are using. They also come to EducationUSA to ask for agent referrals.

EducationUSA was actually prohibited from working with agents when the State Department issued a policy barring it from doing so in 2009. After NACAC permitted incentive compensation, the State Department relaxed its own policy beginning in 2018 to allow agents to participate in EducationUSA events and meetings. EducationUSA has come a long way since then, even sponsoring a special networking session for higher education professionals interested in working with agents at its 2021 Forum. But the degree to which the EducationUSA advising centers integrate agents into their activities depends on each office's priorities. Some have fully integrated them, while others are reluctant to do so.

Prior to the policy change, Jina loosely collaborated with agents at arm's length as "information partners," by informally connecting with the leadership of the Korea Overseas Study Association to share insights and trends about South Korean students. Once the State Department's prohibitive policy was relaxed, Jina saw an opportunity to raise the study abroad industry's level of professionalism. She was inspired by her counterparts at advising centers in other countries who hold training sessions for agents and have frank conversations with them about the ethics of their practice. Her colleagues in the South Korea office, however, frowned upon working with such for-profit entities so brazenly. So Jina integrated agents into her work in ways that are still mindful of her colleagues' reluctancy. She doesn't work with agents directly, but she provides guidance to students on what to look for when seeking out an agent, which she pulls from NACAC's best practices materials. Ultimately, Jina sees agents as cooperative partners who work in alignment with the mission of EducationUSA.

In reality, they don't necessarily have to be a competitor, because if we're sending students to the United States, we really shouldn't be competing. They also fill a gap that we can't. Because if you look at fifty thousand students coming from Korea alone, around that number, what if they all went to EducationUSA? That would be a huge problem. If even a thousand students came to EducationUSA, then we'd have a problem. So I think we recognize that they were there, they're not going anywhere, and they're not necessarily evil. They're doing a job, and sometimes doing a job very well.

As the COVID-19 pandemic has forced Jina and her colleagues to work virtually, they have had to pivot a number of times. They ran their education fairs virtually and used social media much more heavily for their new campaigns. She believed that this has created positive changes overall. She and her colleagues are now much more tech savvy and have gained a better understanding of their workflows and processes. She told me that working under unusual conditions has also made her more intentional about why she does what she does and how important her job is in promoting American interests overseas.

There is the economic side of it . . . The [higher education] industry is bigger than soybeans. Like, we're bigger than soybeans. It's a forty-billion-dollar industry . . . So there's the economic side of it. But then there's just the cultural diplomacy side, which is, I think, the main thing. Which is why it's under the Department of State. That's why it's in embassies. I mean, it's not just a commercial thing . . . That's genuinely something that we think about, that it's a powerful diplomatic currency, diplomatic tool. You're a Fulbrighter. You know this. Cultural understanding and all that stuff. I don't have to explain. It's really the most important thing.

Cultural understanding is certainly important, I agreed, but then I inquired about the political situation in the United States and its impact on her work. Jina was unfazed. She pointed out that South Korea remains relatively unaffected by changing political tides in the United States and that South Korean students have no issue obtaining a visa. Her work has also remained largely unaffected by

Republican or Democratic administrations. In fact, Jina mentioned that during the Trump administration, budgetary allocations for her office actually increased. But perceptions have certainly changed. She fielded more questions from US school representatives wondering whether students will want to come and from South Korean students wondering whether they will be able to go.

Not long after Jina and I talked, major changes happened in the United States. President Biden was inaugurated in January 2021. Six months later, the Departments of State and Education issued the Joint Statement of Principles in Support of International Education. The Statement outlines a clear commitment across federal agencies to support international students studying in the United States, marking what appears to be the first coordinated national approach to international student recruitment.[31] The sudden shift from discoordination to unification from the most sought-after country for students certainly points to the rapidly changing landscape of global higher education.

A Symbiotic Ecosystem

The five stakeholders whom I profile in this chapter work within very different functional areas of the global higher education industry. What connects them is their vested interest in international student mobility outcomes between Berkeley, Seoul, and beyond. Often these individuals have no formal affiliation with the universities to which they direct students, but nonetheless they are part of universities' student recruitment practices. Each stakeholder navigates unique industry pressures as they shape students' choices to pursue higher learning abroad or at home. These individuals from across different facets of the global higher education industry also reap the benefits of students' choices through a symbiotic ecosystem of market-driven rewards.

At the center of the ecosystem is the education agent, who operates as a for-profit broker within a highly commercialized study abroad industry in South Korea. The primary motivation of agents is clearly monetary. They profit from the global aspirations of South Korean youth in their college admissions endeavors, as well as the global aspirations of universities in their quest to enter global student markets. In their customer-facing role, agents negotiate their own ethical standards with those of their customers that are not always aligned. In their business-facing role, agents enter into contractual arrangements with schools to funnel students into novel admissions pipelines. Yet even under pressure to compromise or turn a profit, agents such as Hyeonsuk still seek out a community of like-minded individuals who are connected by more than a desire for dividends. They are also familiar with disruption, and they hedge the risks of their profession with the knowledge that their services will remain valuable as long as they are flexible enough to meet shifting demands.

The agent's counterpart is the admissions recruiter, who functions as an official representative of colleges and universities. Often recruiters enter into contractual relationships with schools that are as flexible as an agent's. Their success depends on bringing in more students for the schools that employ them. Their value is in their vast network of agents within an industry that is highly relationship based. On one level, recruiters like John work rather agnostically, as they juggle multiple contracts and recruit students based on a profit-driven reward system. Yet John clearly believes in the mission of the schools that he represents as he hustles to meet enrollment targets. By meeting these enrollment targets, he believes he is helping both himself and the students whom he funnels to colleges and universities.

On the secondary education side are special purpose high schools in South Korea, which also have a vested interest in where students go to college but from the sending side. The individuals most directly involved in this work are high school guidance counselors. They do not take anything directly from the outcome, but the reputation of

The Global Student Supply Chain   155

their employer becomes part of their calculations as they direct students toward schools that will increase the prestige of the sending high school. But guidance counselors like Gayeong are primarily educators, not admissions professionals, and their own knowledge of the admissions process may be insufficient to meet the exacting demands of students and parents. They work in tandem with education agents, even if only tacitly, because agents fulfill a need for the guidance counselors as well. The goals of both parties are clearly aligned.

As more stakeholders become involved in college admissions, a complex regulatory environment has emerged that establishes best practices across the industry. Professional associations that do this work have tremendous influence, but they ultimately lack the ability to enforce any standards, thus rendering them quasi-regulatory bodies that must themselves navigate a contested ethical terrain. Individuals such as Rob, who have worked within and beyond the regulatory environment, may have misgivings about the efficacy of current regulatory measures. Still, they believe in the value of the work itself and promote ethical standards to the best of their ability.

Meanwhile, governmental bodies that do have enforcement capability have not clearly defined their own goals. In the United States, different federal agencies can operate with different directives about international students, a point that was made painfully clear amid the COVID-19 pandemic. Yet rank-and-file members of the federal workforce such as Jina remained fairly steadfast in continuing their work of promoting American higher education overseas and encouraging more international students to come to the United States, even when messaging from the highest authority of the US government signaled otherwise. And though their reasons for doing so may differ, they also work in tandem with education agents because the end result benefits both parties.

These stakeholders further capitalize on students' global aspirations, even if guided by different motivations, which creates a delicate alignment across what otherwise may appear to be parties in conflict. Monetary compensation facilitates the complex workings of this symbiotic ecosystem, which is why their work is often vilified. But not every individual is motivated solely by profits, and even those who are still emphasize a personal code of ethics as they meet the demands of commoditization. Nonetheless, each actor is merely a single node within an expansive network that sorts students in one direction or another for the benefit of the universities where they enroll.

Summary

Education agents, admissions recruiters, special purpose high schools, quasi-regulatory bodies, and governmental agencies help ensure the global student supply chain runs smoothly between Berkeley and Seoul. Industry insiders who work across different functional areas of global higher education may have a strong sense of personal ethics, but their work is often removed from the universities to which they direct students, as they are part of an expansive ecosystem designed to meet the demands of commoditization. Ultimately, the larger ecosystem that reinforces the global student supply chain is an extension of universities' flexible reach designed to further capitalize on students' global aspirations.

6

Lessons from a Turbulent Decade

The 2010s were a turbulent decade. In the aftermath of the Great Recession, universities all around the world underwent rapid transformations. They fundamentally shifted their priorities to expand into global student markets under financial duress. And the students who attended them during this period were caught in the swirls of those transformations.

What can we extrapolate from the postrecession decade in global higher education? Drawing from a decade of research on universities in Berkeley and Seoul, I have told the story of what happens when universities turn to international students as a solution to budgetary woes. They reformed their existing mechanisms into flexible arrangements to better attract them, which in turn created the very pathways that allowed students to be internationally mobile. I have also shared the story of the South Korean students who attended these universities during this fraught era of higher education reform. These students encountered hostility exactly because their university framed their increasing presence on campus as a financial decision.

Lessons from the Past

While this book is by no means a universal story, what emerges are three important lessons that contribute to our understanding of international student mobility: the emergence of novel pathways; the contested influx of international students; and the acknowledgment of the global student supply chain.

The Emergence of Novel Pathways

Universities in Berkeley and Seoul created novel pathways for international students to enter. At UC Berkeley, international students became a financial impetus for an institution that found itself in a budget crisis, resulting in the university increasing international student enrollments. But domestic pushback to their more visible presence on campus eventually restricted their numbers across the UC schools. And as selective universities such as UC Berkeley restricted international enrollments, neighboring community colleges strategically positioned themselves as accessible transfer gateways for students who may not have been admitted right away. These colleges were able to use their accessibility as a marketing tool and capitalize on the global aspirations of students from outside the United States exactly because the UC schools restricted their access. Seen in this way, the California higher education system as a whole could continue to facilitate entryways for international students even as some institutions created barriers to entry.

Meanwhile, Yonsei University launched an international college intended to attract international students as a way to bypass a governmental quota of domestic students the university was allowed to enroll. The college adopted an American liberal arts curriculum, taught entirely in English, by American faculty members recruited from overseas. But when international student numbers did not meet expectations, the university repurposed its international college to retain globally minded domestic students. The learning environment found at an international college housed inside a South Korean university offered these students an alternative to studying in the United States that capitalized on their global aspirations. It also still enabled Yonsei to bypass a governmental quota of domestic students the university was allowed to enroll by creating a special admissions track for a subset of domestic students deemed "international" under governmental exemptions.

Though situated in entirely different contexts, these two universities similarly vied for a greater share of global student markets. Each context determined how they did so—indeed, whether a university was located in a receiving or sending country of students determined this—and created the conditions for international student mobility flows to proliferate. These two universities also contended with domestic realities that limited their ability to admit more students under governmental restrictions. As a result, they forged novel pathways that bypassed such restrictions and still enabled international (or "international") students to enter.

These examples indicate how scholars and practitioners must engage with more nuanced understandings of international student mobility flows beyond single-country case studies to make sense of the postrecession decade in global higher education. They must also examine how universities recruit international students by putting into conversation institutions in receiving countries with institutions in sending countries. How do universities across both contexts increase their share of global student markets? What novel pathways are created when universities reconcile their own global aspirations with their domestic realities?

The Contested Influx of International Students

As universities in Berkeley and Seoul created novel pathways for international students to enter, they also created special admissions standards for their particular version of the international student. At UC Berkeley, international students were framed as a necessary financial solution to a budget crisis but excluded from any diversity rhetoric. This led to the California higher education system aggressively seeking out international students across community colleges while restricting their access at selective universities such as UC Berkeley, where there was—and still is—significant domestic pushback. It was the opposite at Yonsei, where international students were prioritized in the admissions process for their perceived globality, and by the same token, assumed to increase prestige for a university that itself aspired to global status. This led to Yonsei categorizing a subset of domestic students as "international" because of their English fluency and time spent overseas in order to justify the novel learning space that they occupied and the higher tuition that they paid. These different frames nonetheless share the assumption that international students are exceptionally affluent and uninhibitedly mobile and will bring dividends for the universities that can attract them.

"Those rich international students" have thus come to represent a zero-sum admissions competition because of the unusual pathways afforded to them. And at selective institutions such as UC Berkeley and Yonsei, the competition among hopeful students is fierce. Yet South Korean students who pursued unconventional pathways leading to UC Berkeley or Yonsei were able to take advantage of universities' flexible arrangements and bypass more unforgiving admissions tracks. The ones who did so were by no means less capable, and many had already pursued early study abroad and other forms of global learning that prepared them well for higher learning at one institution or another. But as a result, these students faced discrimination by their peers exactly because of the unusual way in which they entered their university. Their contested status as "transfer students" at UC Berkeley or "foreign students" at Yonsei—terms that suggest that they gained admission by virtue of their globality and wealth—rendered them illegitimate and colored their experiences on campus.

The interplay between international student recruitment and international student experiences highlights how student life is inseparable from the institutional configurations of the universities where students enroll. To this end, scholars and practitioners must examine the student experience with a thorough understanding of the organizational behavior of universities. What are the consequences of international student recruitment practices on the students themselves? How are students' understandings and sensibilities shaped by the very universities that brought them there in the first place?

Notably, the greatest backlash to South Korean students at UC Berkeley and Yonsei came from other South Korean students, who ostracized members of their own community as they themselves internalized harmful discourses around international students. They wielded racialized stereotypes about international students generally against members of their own community as a way to protect themselves from becoming the targets. They were also affected by increasing economic precarity and decreasing return on investment on their university degree, which led to them creating new competitive advantages for themselves by creating new markers of legitimacy around how they gained admission.

Such intricate student relations point to the complex intraethnic tensions around the influx of international students that must also be considered alongside interethnic ones. For example, research on the influx of Mainland Chinese students at Singaporean and Hong Kong universities reveals new tensions emerging among those broadly labeled as Chinese.[1] While there is abundant research on intercultural tensions surrounding the influx of international students broadly, scholars and practitioners must develop more nuanced understandings that go beyond a conventional frame of domestic versus international. How do notions of globality and wealth create divisions within international student communities? What are the variegated experiences even among international students from the same country?

Acknowledging the Global Student Supply Chain

Finally, as we have seen, global higher education not only is about universities or the students who attend them but also encompasses a vast array of stakeholders—including education agents, admissions recruiters, special purpose high schools, quasi-regulatory bodies, and governmental agencies. Each stakeholder negotiates larger industry pressures with its own motivations and goals as it capitalizes on students' global aspirations. Collectively, they help ensure the global student supply chain runs smoothly as they channel students in one direction or another within a market-driven reward system.

Acknowledging the global student supply chain raises important questions about how scholars and practitioners understand the university's global reach. Often a stakeholder does not even have a formal relationship to a university but is firmly entrenched within the university's student recruitment practices. This phenomenon requires further mapping of the supply chain across transnational contexts to make sense of the expansive ecosystem that is global higher education.

Acknowledging the global student supply chain also means acknowledging that students are no longer just customers but also commodities. It ascribes much more agency on the part of universities and the ancillary people and organizations that work in tandem with them to capitalize on students' global aspirations. It also calls into question whether students really have much of a choice when they study abroad because their choices are compelled by numerous external parties. By changing the narrative that students are commodities rather than customers, scholars and practitioners can ask more pointed questions about who, exactly, benefits from them. Beyond universities, who also gains from the proliferation of international student mobility flows, and by what means? How can we establish the boundaries around where one stakeholder's student recruitment practices begin and another's end?

In the Aftermath of the COVID-19 Pandemic

In the aftermath of the COVID-19 pandemic, competition for international students will certainly intensify, as will domestic constraints to their ability to enroll. In receiving countries like the United States, lingering Trumpism and general wariness from the pandemic will lead to universities reconfiguring their arrangements into even more novel pathways that still allow international students to enter but are mindful of domestic pushback. These schools toe a delicate line between expanding into global student markets and bowing to domestic pressures that fixate on international students as drivers of inequity. They do so by imagining new products that create not only the pathways that allow students to be internationally mobile but also the global student markets that would not have existed otherwise. For example, ventures into adult education and online education—of which I am a part of through my work at Georgetown University—upend notions of international students as young and mobile and capitalize on the global aspirations of a new crop of students who are older and more settled. And these novel pathways will continue to generate domestic pushback around who deserves entry into selective universities.

Likewise, universities in sending countries across Asia will also continue to reconfigure their arrangements into novel pathways that disrupt international student mobility flows to receiving countries like the United States. As we have seen, higher education reform efforts in South Korea present a dynamic picture of how universities can actively reverse outbound flows. A similar scenario is unfolding in China. Already, we can see the number of Chinese students in the United States plateauing as Chinese universities also benefit from national funding schemes and transform their existing arrangements to capitalize on Chinese students' global aspirations. But even as international student mobility flows from Asia to the United States will likely wane, we will continue to see "American-style" higher learning proliferate across Asian universities. The creation of these new learning spaces that reappropriate the American learning model in unexpected contexts will also continue to generate complex intraethnic tensions around a new generation of students who may not study abroad but will certainly experience American higher education.

Beyond universities, the many stakeholders across the global higher education industry will only become nimbler in the face of extreme disruption. Many have already experienced dramatic setbacks to the global student supply chain, whether it was the Asian financial crisis of the late 1990s or the global financial crisis of the late 2000s. And as survival within this industry demands a greater ability to weather volatility, smaller players will face disadvantages while larger conglomerates, such as pathway providers and agent aggregators, will proliferate.

The Present Aftermath

Students from South Korea were able to pursue higher learning in Berkeley and Seoul as their universities created the very pathways that allowed them to enter. Their experiences may have been unique to the postrecession decade in higher education, but the aftermath of those experiences resonates today. How did these students fare in their postcollege lives? I followed up with Jessica, Audrey, and Yuri to find out.

Jessica

When I first met Jessica, a student at UC Berkeley, in 2017, she used a strategy of omission to obscure the way in which she gained admission as a community college transfer student from De Anza College. She knew that having attended a community college would stigmatize her among her peers. Her personal strategy mirrored her college's strategy of international student recruitment, which aggressively promoted its transfer opportunities as a tactical, even furtive, pathway to a more selective university. Jessica had isolated herself socially while at De Anza because she believed she would move on to better opportunities. Only when she became a student at UC Berkeley did she allow herself to become more socially integrated, eventually becoming one of the most visible leaders of the Korean student community on campus.

Years later, I reconnected with Jessica to see what she was up to. She had graduated from UC Berkeley as a political economy major in 2018. Upon graduating, she focused on applying to graduate schools and enrolled in a master's program in public policy the following year at the University of Chicago. She wanted to experience another part of the United States and was drawn to Chicago's reputation as an academically rigorous school, she told me. By the time we spoke again in 2021, Jessica had recently graduated from the master's program and was in the middle of her job search. Still the same self-assured woman whom I met in Berkeley, she talked extensively about the kind of job that she was looking for—specifically, in the finance or private equity sector—and how she was waiting for the "right" offer to come her way, even turning down ones that didn't meet her high standards. Though she still aspired to work in her father's import-export business in South Korea someday, she wanted to prove her abilities by first starting her career in the United States on her own.

Most immediately, Jessica expressed a strong desire to move back to the San Francisco Bay Area, where she spent her formative years as a college student and where she felt most comfortable. Most unexpectedly, she expressed a strong nostalgia for her time not necessarily at UC Berkeley but at De Anza. It was, in hindsight, where she felt she had learned the skills to become the confident woman she is. At her community college, Jessica was afforded the opportunity to learn how to be independent and succeed in a competitive environment, which prepared her well for her subsequent academic success at UC Berkeley and Chicago. She expressed gratitude for this, which was a surprising departure from how she framed her education at a community college in an inferior way when we first connected years ago.

Jessica's story shows what happens when international students are pitted against domestic students in a zero-sum admissions competition. She encountered hostility at UC Berkeley because the California higher education system ambiguously values international students for their tuition dollars but otherwise deems them detrimental to the system's public mission. This "us versus them" framing of international students has created a bifurcated admissions process, in which California community colleges aggressively recruit more international students while the UC system imposes strict quotas on their enrollment. Notably, Jessica faced the strongest enmity from other South Korean students. International students themselves have internalized the messaging that they are valued only as financial assets and transposed the stereotype of "those rich international students" onto members of their own community. But this zero-sum admissions competition is not inevitable—in fact, economists have shown otherwise—but rather a racialized form of scapegoating for shrinking university budgets that harms bright and motivated students like Jessica.[2]

Audrey

What struck me about Audrey, a student at Yonsei, when we first met in 2012 was how she seemingly fit the image of the wealthy, global student that universities clamor to attract. Born in Seoul and raised in Turkey with a cosmopolitan upbringing that included international schools across Europe, she returned to South Korea as a college student to refamiliarize herself with her country of citizenship. She enrolled at Yonsei's Underwood International College because it was a learning environment that could accommodate her worldly background, according to her. It was also one of the few institutions in South Korea that offered an all-English learning environment that was more comfortable for her.

A lot had happened by the time Audrey and I reconnected. After she graduated from Yonsei in 2012, she spent six months in Egypt to study Arabic and then returned to Seoul to work as a news assistant at the South Korean branch of an international news agency. She continued that work until she was eventually offered her dream job of doing humanitarian work in the Middle East. She joined an international humanitarian organization in 2015 and then lived and worked across the region—in Pakistan, Afghanistan, and Northern Iraq—where she provided humanitarian aid to refugees. Assigned to another part of Iraq when we spoke again in 2021, she talked at length about her passion for helping displaced populations, which in many ways mirrored her own childhood as a "third culture kid." Interestingly, she emphasized how living and working among a global group of other humanitarian workers as an adult inspired her to identify more strongly as a South Korean, which was a departure from how she distinguished herself from "a typical Korean" in her college days.

Audrey has become something of a model citizen for her alma mater. Whenever she returns to Seoul to visit her family, she is invited to give talks at Yonsei and share her career trajectory with current students. Indeed, she has become a model citizen not just for her university but for her country, which prominently features her in government-sponsored promotional videos that tout the humanitarian contributions that South Korea has made. This was certainly a surprising development for an alumna of an international college who was ostracized by her Yonsei peers for being too "foreign" only a decade ago.

Audrey's story shows how newer patterns of international student mobility challenge the primacy of the United States in global higher education—but not because it is losing students to other English-speaking countries. Audrey's enrollment at Yonsei's international college is a clear indication of how universities in South Korea have become attractive, even preferable, options for globally minded South Korean students. This adds another dimension to our understanding of competition in the global student marketplace. The prevailing understanding across the US higher education community is that international students come from Asian countries and study in Western ones. Hence, the assumption is that US universities must compete with universities in places like Canada or Australia for these internationally mobile students. But reflecting on Audrey's story, we should not be asking why students choose to study abroad in one country or another; rather, we should be asking why some students choose not to study abroad in the first place. Many South Korean students do not study abroad exactly because South Korean universities have made substantial efforts to recruit students from within their own borders and reverse the outflow of domestic students. Shrinking numbers of students from important sending countries such as South Korea reveal newer patterns of international student mobility that decenter the United States and its supposed competitors.

Yuri

At Yonsei University, I also met Yuri. When we met in 2012, Yuri had recently returned from an exchange year in Switzerland and was in her last year of college, majoring in political science. Yuri was quite different from Audrey, her close friend, when they began college. Yuri was a local student from Seoul, while Audrey was a transnational returnee from Turkey, but they formed a strong bond because they shared the unique experience of learning together within Yonsei's Underwood International College. They also faced social rejection by students from the rest of Yonsei. This simultaneous inclusion and exclusion was the result of an international college's ambiguous positional strategy within the larger university in which it was housed. The college promoted its special curriculum as a distinctly global experience while recruiting mostly domestic students who may or may not have sought an international education but certainly sought admission into a selective university in South Korea.

Reconnecting with Yuri also revealed unexpected developments. After Yuri returned from her year abroad in Switzerland in 2012, her Swiss boyfriend followed her to South Korea by becoming an exchange student at Yonsei. He eventually returned to Switzerland, and a year later, Yuri graduated from Yonsei. She took on odd jobs, such as teaching English at a hagwon, but missed him considerably. So she took a bold step and moved to Switzerland later that year to reconnect with her beau. There, she pursued a second bachelor's degree and, subsequently, a master's degree in art history at the University of Zurich. When we reconnected in 2021, she was nearing completion of the master's program and preparing to work as an art curator. She seemed happy with her life in Switzerland, where she had married her partner in 2017 and intended to stay permanently. By then, she was a fluent speaker of Korean, English, and German with an advanced degree from an overseas university. She herself had transformed into a member of the cosmopolitan elite by whom she was quite intimidated by when she first entered Yonsei.

Indeed, Yuri talked at length about how becoming globally oriented herself has made her rethink her interactions with transnational returnees when she was a college student at Yonsei. But she had also experienced much personal tension with her parents, whom she had described as "typical Korean parents" both in her college days and when we spoke again. Her parents did not understand her life choices, she told me. Yuri's younger brother had gotten a job in South Korea and married a South Korean, and her parents wondered why Yuri did not do the same. But she found solace in maintaining a close friendship with Audrey, whose own transnational life was certainly an inspiration.

Yuri's story is a prime example of how some students are transformed by the novel pathways afforded them by their university. Yuri had never intended to study abroad, and she enrolled at an international college as a strategic way to enter Yonsei. She was hardly different from other domestic students who graduated from local high schools and entered the university for the same reasons. But once she studied at an international college, she was immersed in a novel curriculum and developed close friendships with students like Audrey. Living abroad was once unimaginable for Yuri, but eventually she spent a year abroad as an exchange student during college and later became a global nomad herself, in no small part because of her unique learning environment and exposure to friends who had those experiences. Yuri's story shows just how influential her university was in shaping who she became, in college and beyond.

Constructing Student Mobility

Ultimately, these three students became the internationally mobile individuals their universities assumed them to be. Their universities recruited them because of their presumed globality and wealth. As a result, they encountered and internalized harmful stereotypes about "those rich international students" on their campuses. They also adjusted to the academic and social expectations of their learning environments that prepared them for transnational careers afterwards, whether or not they were inclined to pursue them. Their lives in college and beyond followed the pathways their universities constructed in order to bring them there in the first place.

Pondering the Future of International Student Mobility

In the second year of the COVID-19 pandemic, I spoke over Zoom with a close friend, Jiyeong. Jiyeong lives and works in Seoul. I had hoped to see her there in the summer of 2021, but the continuing pandemic prevented me from traveling. Instead, over Zoom, she shared updates about her job and her family. She also sent me a link to a video that piqued my interest. In the video, red and green holiday decorations flank a small stage where four-year-old children act out a nativity scene and sing and dance to "Jingle Bells" and "Winter Wonderland." Bemused parents watch from the audience and smile and clap for their children. It was a scene from a preschool's winter concert featured in its promotional video to parents of prospective students. The preschool was Sookmyung Kinder Academy, a private preschool in Seoul that specializes in English immersion for children ages two to six. The South Korean children participating in the winter concert were already speaking—nay, acting and performing on stage—fluently in American-accented English.

After a year on a waitlist to get into Sookmyung, Jiyeong's toddler son was able to take a highly coveted spot. Jiyeong pays around $1,000 per month to send him there, an expense that she and her husband, both professors, are able to budget. They wanted to ensure that their son attained not just the English language prerequisites but also the naturalness and fluency of English that would enable him to thrive in a global environment, she told me.

Jiyeong and her husband are part of an earlier cohort of South Korean millennials born in the early 1980s and among the large wave of South Koreans to pursue their higher education in the United States in the 2000s and early 2010s. These early millennials were some of the most outwardly mobile students in the world. They both attended graduate school in California, which is how they met (and how I met them). Jiyeong has since completed her education abroad and returned to South Korea, and her overseas education positioned her well for her high-powered job. But she and her husband felt that they had struggled with language barriers while in the United States because they had not studied abroad earlier. Indeed, Jiyeong's sister, who is a decade younger, studied in the United States as a high school student and an undergraduate and is evidence to Jiyeong of the benefits of English immersion at an earlier age. So she and her husband made an intentional decision to send their son to an

English immersion preschool. Upon enrolling him, they met other South Korean millennial parents with former study abroad experience who hold the same global aspirations for their children.

Another year later, in 2022, I began to resume activities I had paused at the onset of the pandemic. I started traveling again, and I flew to Seoul for a couple weeks in the summer to reconnect with friends and colleagues. I was overjoyed to be able to see Jiyeong in person. We met at a tea house in the Insadong area. As she shared further updates about her job and family, I was struck by how much time had passed since I had last seen her. No longer a toddler, her son was in his last year at Sookmyung, and Jiyeong was faced with a difficult decision. She had to decide whether to continue his English immersion at an even more specialized primary school, where the tuition is double that of Sookmyung. She was also considering spending her upcoming sabbatical at a US university so that she could bring her son for early study abroad in the United States. Concerned about whether the financial costs to educate her son would pay off, she asked me, a scholar who studies this very phenomenon, what I thought.

If this book is about students like Jiyeong and the universities that allowed them to be internationally mobile, then her son and schools like Sookmyung are poised to become the next permutation of this phenomenon. Indeed, as former international students from South Korea are themselves becoming parents, their own educational backgrounds certainly influence the choices they make for their children. By enrolling her son at Sookmyung, Jiyeong is able to take advantage of an exclusive learning opportunity for him beginning as early as preschool. Yet even Jiyeong, an overseas-educated professor at one of the most prestigious universities in Seoul, was concerned about whether her son would attain the same advantages as she has had. Her hopes and anxieties for her son's future were intertwined with an understanding that previously novel pathways to higher learning and economic success are no longer that novel. Meanwhile, highly specialized schools such as Sookmyung capitalize on the evolving aspirations of former international students, now themselves parents of children pursuing even more novel pathways than their parents did.

What future pathways await this new generation of students, I wondered. While I did not have a concrete answer, I could sense that Jiyeong needed one. But it's one thing to analyze international student mobility as a scholar; it's an entirely different situation to give a close friend parenting advice. After a brief pause, I reassured her that whatever she decides to do, her son would be well cared for. Then I pulled out a gift I had prepared, a Georgetown University children's sized t-shirt for her son. Jiyeong smiled.

Methodological Appendix

As I discussed in the opening chapter, this book is the cumulative product of three distinct research projects. What follows is a discussion of my research process for each of those projects, presented in chronological order.

Project 1 (2011–2012)

From 2011 to 2012, while I was a doctoral student, I lived in Seoul for twelve months while affiliated with Yonsei University as an international exchange student. During this time, I conducted an institutional ethnography of Underwood International College (UIC), which is part of Yonsei, for my dissertation. The project sought to uncover the role of an international college within the larger South Korean university in which it is housed by understanding the institutional arrangements that connect the people within it.

As an international exchange student at Yonsei, I had full access to campus resources. I used this opportunity to immerse myself in the daily life of a student by taking courses, attending school events, and mingling with other students in order to investigate firsthand the student experience at the university. Additionally, I conducted forty-eight semistructured interviews with students, faculty members, and senior administrators at UIC and throughout Yonsei. My questions were tailored to each individual's specific role but followed a general guideline. The interviews took place on and off campus, in offices, and over coffee or lunch, and lasted approximately one to three hours in an oral interview format, with the exception of one interview conducted over multiple email communications. All of the questions were given in English; however, some individuals responded to some or all of them in Korean, or incorporated Korean words or phrases within their English responses. All interviews were recorded and transcribed, unless an individual had requested otherwise.

Over time, several individuals emerged as key informants, including those who worked for the university. I connected with them multiple times to clarify concepts or verify information about the inner workings of their department. To avoid jeopardizing anyone's employment status within Yonsei, any faculty members whom I interviewed were given the opportunity to review the interview transcript and request that I not use specific quotes or comments. I also interviewed administrative leaders (e.g., deans, associate deans, board members), including the founders of the international college. These individuals spoke to me from their leadership role within the university. Hence, I interpreted what they shared with me as comments indicative of the views of the institution, as opposed to their personal views, and represented them as such. These and other ethical considerations of the project were overseen by the Institutional Review Board at UCLA.

Following my time in Seoul, I kept in contact with some of the Yonsei students over email and social media. I reached out to the ones whom I've featured prominently in this book and re-interviewed them over Zoom in 2021. In our follow-up discussions, I informed them of my intention to highlight their stories and asked them to tell me about their postcollege lives in a more unstructured interview, which I recorded and transcribed.

Project 2 (2016–2017)

After completing my PhD, I worked at UC Berkeley for four years, first as a postdoctoral scholar and then an administrative staff member. Because I was working in a full-time job that required me to be on campus every day, I was unable to engage in extensive periods of overseas fieldwork like I had done as a doctoral student. I began to think of my immediate surroundings as a research site, since it was a way that I could stay active in scholarship while in an alternative academic position.

As the program director of the Center for Korean Studies, I was frequently around South Koreans, whether it was international students enrolled at UC Berkeley, visiting scholars affiliated with the Center, or the myriad of people who passed through for talks and conferences. Through my proximity to South Korean students, I learned about the community college transfer pipeline into UC Berkeley and the significance it had for the Korean student community. Through my many conversations and shared meals with South Korean scholars, I became intimately aware of the lengths to which parents will go to pursue study abroad opportunities for their children, especially as their own overseas pursuits were often entangled with their children's.

At the same time, I was putting on talks and conferences nearly every week at the Center, many of which were on topics that I likely wouldn't have paid much attention to had it not been for my job. By engaging with the wide gamut of interdisciplinary scholarship—and the scholars themselves—that constitute Asian studies, I became familiar with major debates happening across disciplines quite far from my own. I was particularly struck by the interdisciplinary literature on students, which often centered on the students while largely ignoring what was happening within the universities where they enrolled. This felt incongruous to me as a staff member at UC Berkeley, where I was booking flights, processing visas, and transferring funds to bring South Koreans to the campus for one reason or another.

These experiences became the genesis for this book, which emphasizes the role of the university in our understanding of international student mobility. From 2016 to 2017, while I continued to work at UC Berkeley, I went about an institutional ethnography of UC Berkeley that sought to contextualize the South Korean student experience at a campus with a sudden influx of international students. At UC Berkeley, I attended school events, visited student clubs, and pored through student newspapers and online forums. I also conducted twenty semistructured interviews with South Korean students enrolled at UC Berkeley and nearby community colleges. The interviews took place on and off campus, in campus common areas, at the library, and in coffeeshops and cafes, and lasted approximately one to three hours in an oral interview format. All of the questions were given in English; however, some individuals responded to some or all of them in Korean, or incorporated Korean words or phrases within their English responses. All interviews were recorded and transcribed.

My position allowed me to easily meet students to interview, and I tried to stay conscious of power dynamics that would affect the interview. Thus, I mostly interviewed students with whom I did not have a direct working relationship nor were in any of the courses that I taught. These and other ethical considerations of the project were overseen by the Institutional Review Board at UC Berkeley.

After leaving UC Berkeley and developing some distance to my work there, I was able to draw connections between the themes that emerged from this project with those that emerged from the prior one I had conducted at Yonsei. The unexpected parallels I discovered became the inspiration for the methodological framework that I adopt that focuses on the university as the primary actor in global higher education. As I did with select Yonsei students, I also reached out to the UC Berkeley students whom I've featured prominently in this book and re-interviewed them over Zoom in 2021. In our follow-up discussions, I informed them of my intention to highlight their stories and asked them to tell me about their postcollege lives in a more unstructured interview, which I recorded and transcribed.

Project 3 (2020–2021)

I continued to develop the methodological framework for this book while drafting early chapters. Meanwhile, I began working at Georgetown University as a professor of the practice (another name for a nontenure track faculty member) in the School of Continuing Studies. Teaching in a master's program in higher education administration brought me back to my disciplinary training in education. As the inaugural faculty director of the master's program, I was also charged with launching the program, developing the curriculum, and growing enrollment.

Indeed, my job hinged on healthy enrollment in the master's program. This opened up a new avenue of anxiety but also creativity. During the launch phase, much of my work involved collaborating with admissions and marketing professionals to find ways to attract students. I became equal parts scholar, teacher, and marketeer, often blurring the distinctions, such as when I would teach sample classes to prospective students or design academic events in conjunction with the marketing team to get the word out about the master's program. This was in stark contrast to the higher education scholarship that I was familiar with and regularly taught to my students, which frequently railed against capitalist encroachment into university life.

I wondered whether there could be a more nuanced way to contextualize the practical conditions under which many individuals work within higher education. At the same time, I realized that there was a critical piece missing from my book that focused on universities and the students who attend them. My own work demanded that I work closely with people who have a stronger background in business than in education, or organizations that have only loose connections with universities. I became more familiar with the vast world of higher education beyond universities involved in student recruitment—an area that was quite under-researched by scholars.

From 2020 to 2021, while I continued to work at Georgetown University, I conducted a qualitative narrative inquiry of student recruitment professionals in order to understand the different facets of the global higher education industry involved in international student mobility between the United States and South Korea. I attended student recruitment fairs, observed student recruitment practices in person and virtually, and had numerous informal chats with student recruitment professionals. I also conducted fifteen semistructured interviews with industry insiders, including education agents, admissions recruiters, and those who work in special purpose high schools, quasi-regulatory bodies, and governmental agencies. I connected with these individuals through the contacts I cultivated through my work and through former classmates from graduate school, some of whom were now working in this industry. Interviews were conducted in either English or Korean, depending on the speaker's preferred language, and were recorded and transcribed. The ethical considerations of the project were overseen by the Institutional Review Board at Georgetown.

Notes

1 "Those Rich International Students"

1. Ong, *Neoliberalism as Exception.*

2. NAFSA, "United States of America."

3. NAFSA, "United States."

4. For example, see Fong, *Paradise Redefined*; Ma, *Ambitious and Anxious*; Waters and Brooks, *Student Migrants*; and Martin, *Dreams of Flight.*

5. This approach is called methodological nationalism. For further discussion, see Shahjahan and Kezar, "Beyond the 'National Container.'"

6. For further discussion on vertical case studies in comparative education research, see Vavrus and Bartlett, eds., *Critical Approaches to Comparative Education.*

7. For further discussion on the different waves of international students in the United States, see Choudaha, "Third Wave of International Student Mobility."

8. Thelin, *History of American Higher Education.*

9. Slaughter and Leslie, *Academic Capitalism.*

10. Slaughter and Rhoades, *Academic Capitalism.*

11. Hazelkorn, *Rankings and Reshaping of Higher Education.*

12. Altbach and Knight, "Internationalization of Higher Education."

13. DiMaggio and Powell, "Iron Cage Revisited"; Powell and DiMaggio, eds., *New Institutionalism in Organizational Analysis*; Immergut, "Theoretical Core of the New

Institutionalism"; Dacin, Goodstein, and Scott, "Institutional Theory and Institutional Change."

14. For example, see Fisher, *Education Crossing Borders*.

15. Knight, "Internationalization Remodeled."

16. Stromquist, "Internationalization as a Response."

17. I also recognize other definitions of internationalization that have influenced the field of higher education, including those developed by Hans de Wit and colleagues, and Jenny Lee. See de Wit et al., *Internationalisation of Higher Education*; and Lee, ed., *U.S. Power in International Higher Education*.

18. Hazelkorn, *Rankings and Reshaping of Higher Education*; Wilbers and Brankovic, "The Emergence of University Rankings."

19. For example, in 2020, the Trump administration announced Proclamations 10014, 10052, and 10131 that suspended the processing of immigrant and nonimmigrant visas in order to protect Americans from competition over scarce jobs during the pandemic. These Proclamations have since been revoked by the Biden administration.

20. For an overview of policies that prevented international students from coming to or staying in the United States during the Trump administration, see Kim, "Coming to America."

21. Even prior to the COVID-19 pandemic, hostility against international students from Asian countries had been growing alongside their more visible presence on American campuses. I discuss this in further detail in Chapter 2. See also Yao, " 'They Don't Care About You.' "

22. IIE, *Open Doors*.

23. For example, see Fischer and Aslanian, "Fading Beacon."

24. Sohn, "Ghost Story."

25. Lo et al., *South Korea's Education Exodus*.

26. Lee, "'I Am a Kirogi Mother' "; Finch and Kim, "Kirŏgi Familes in the US."

27. For example, see Collins, *Global Asian City*.

28. Park and Abelmann, "Class and Cosmopolitan Striving."

29. Park and Wee, *Markets of English*.

30. IIE, *Open Doors*.

31. Appadurai, *Modernity at Large*; Shin, *Ethnic Nationalism in Korea*.

32. Moon, "Internationalization without Cultural Diversity?"

33. Cho, "Spec Generation Who Can't"; Chun and Han, "Language Travels and Global Aspirations."

34. Robertson, Cheng, and Yeoh, "Introduction," *Journal of Intercultural Studies.*

35. Waters and Leung, "Immobile Transnationalisms?"

36. Choudaha, "Know Your International Student."

37. Jon, "Realizing Internationalization at Home."

38. For example, see Beech, *Geographies of International Student Mobility*; and Kim and Kwak, eds., *Outward and Upward Mobilities.*

39. In addition to Ortiga's book, see also Ortiga, "Flexible University."

40. Kauppinen, Mathies, and Weimer, "Developing a Conceptual Model," 251. See also Cantwell and Kauppinen, eds., *Academic Capitalism in the Age of Globalization.*

41. Xiang and Lindquist, "Migration Infrastructure."

42. Shrestha and Yeoh, "Introduction."

2   A Pathway into UC Berkeley

1. UC Berkeley, "UC Berkeley Fall Enrollment Data."

2. Kerr, *Uses of the University*, 63–65.

3. UCOP, *Major Features.*

4. UCOP, *Major Features.*

5. Douglass, *Conditions for Admission*, 88.

6. Marginson, *Dream Is Over*, 51–55.

7. Full disclosure: By request of the Center for Studies in Higher Education, I gave occasional lectures to visiting delegations from China for this exact purpose.

8. Douglass, *California Idea*; Douglass, *Conditions for Admission.*

9. Bowles and Gintis, *Schooling in Capitalist America*; Apple, *Education and Power.*

10. Douglass, "University of California Versus the SAT."

11. At the time of writing this book, the University of California eliminated the use of SAT and ACT scores as an admissions requirement for freshman applicants as a result of the decision, appeal, and settlement of Kawika Smith v. Regents of the University of California, 2019 Cal. Sup. RG19046222. However, international students must still submit English proficiency scores, which can include SAT or ACT scores.

12. Gilmore, "In a Pandemic Year."

13. Bady and Konczal, "From Master Plan to No Plan."

14. Cook, *Higher Education Funding.*

15. Bleemer, "Affirmative Action, Mismatch, and Economic Mobility."

16. Park, *Race on Campus.*

17. Poon and Segoshi, "Racial Mascot Speaks."

18. Lee and Zhou, *Asian American Achievement Paradox.*

19. By contrast, the UC schools have a much longer history of accepting international students at the graduate level, especially in the STEM fields.

20. Jaquette and Curs, "Creating the Out-of-State University."

21. UCLA, "Undergraduate Profile."

22. Lee and Rice, "Welcome to America?"

23. UCOP, "UC Board of Regents Approves Policy."

24. Bohn, Reyes, and Johnson, "Impact of Budget Cuts."

25. Bohn, Reyes, and Johnson, "Impact."

26. IIE, "Open Doors."

27. These are the student fees as of Spring 2022. See Santa Monica College, "Tuition, Fees and Payment Deadlines."

28. UCOP, "Admissions by Source School."

29. Raby et al., "International Student Mobility."

30. Lee, "Freshman and Transfer Students."

31. An earlier 2011 article published in *Berkeley Opinion* discusses the terms "freshman students" versus "transfer students" used by South Korean students at UC Berkeley. See Springdale, "Transfer Students."

32. As of the 2020–2021 academic year, students from South Korea are the third-largest group of international students enrolled at community colleges across the United States, trailing students from China and Vietnam. See IIE, "Open Doors."

33. The UC Office of the President and Berkeley International Office do not provide a breakdown of the country of origin among international transfer students within publicly available data. I have estimated the scope of South Korean students among this population by triangulating national-level data with UC Berkeley international student enrollment statistics.

34. Choudaha, Orosz, and Chang, "Not All International Students."

35. These intraethnic tensions are a departure from previous research that revealed intraethnic othering of South Korean students by Korean American students, which I did not find to be the case at UC Berkeley. See Abelmann, *The Intimate University.* Additionally, more recent research shows how international students from China can be racialized as Others while perpetuating the racialization of Black and Brown communities at a predominantly White institution in the United States. See Jiang, "Diversity Without Integration?"

3   A Pathway into Yonsei University

1. Significant portions of this chapter were included in my dissertation. See Kim, "An International College in South Korea as a Third Space." Significant portions of this chapter were also published as a journal article. See Kim, "Illegitimate Elites."

2. Eagleton, "Slow Death of the University."

3. AAC&U, *What Liberal Education Looks Like.*

4. Arum and Roska, *Academically Adrift.*

5. Bok, *Our Underachieving Colleges.*

6. Newfield, *The Great Mistake.*

7. Aronowitz, *Against Schooling.*

8. Jung, Ishimura, and Sasao, eds., *Liberal Arts Education and Colleges in East Asia.*

9. Cheng, "Liberal Arts Educated Citizen."

10. Mok, "Questing for Internationalization of Universities in Asia"; Deem, Mok, and Lucas, "Transforming Higher Education in Whose Image?"

11. Phan, *Transnational Education Crossing "Asia" and "the West."*

12. Chen, *Asia as Method.*

13. Liu and Lye, "Liberal Arts for Asians."

14. For example, see Alexander, *Academia Next.*

15. World Bank Open Data, "Fertility Rate."

16. OECD, *Education at a Glance.*

17. OECD, *Education.*

18. Byun, "Shadow Education and Academic Success."

19. UNESCO Institute for Statistics, "Global Flow of Tertiary-Level Students."

20. UNESCO, "Global Flow"; Carnegie Classification of Institutions of Higher Education, *Carnegie Classification.*

21. KEDI, *Brief Statistics on Korean Education.*

22. Byun and Kim, "Shifting Patterns of Government's Policies."

23. Mo, *Korea's Quest for Global Education*, 29.

24. Looser, "Global University."

25. Mo, *Korea's Quest for Global Education*, 34–37.

26. Mohrman, Ma, and Baker, "Research University in Transition."

27. Beginning in 2014, only advertisements for faculty positions within the college's signature liberal arts program, and select humanities and social science fields, specify a requirement of non–South Korean citizenship.

28. This instrumentalist approach to faculty recruitment cuts both ways. The American faculty members themselves employed what the higher education scholar Terri Kim calls "transnational identity capital," or their embodied positional knowledge from traversing national borders, as a way to assert their special status within Yonsei. See Kim, "Academic Mobility, Transnational Identity Capital, and Stratification." See also Kim, "Western Faculty 'Flight Risk' at Korean University."

29. This is the tuition amount and currency conversion as of Spring 2022. See Underwood International College, "Tuition Fee."

30. The Ministry of Education controls the number of students each university is allowed to enroll through strict quotas. However, in tandem with policies that encourage more international students to study in South Korea, the Ministry has deemed international students exempt. This creates flexibility for universities such as Yonsei to admit as many international students as it wants.

31. Lo and Kim, "Linguistic Competency and Citizenship."

32. Xiang, Yeoh, and Toyota, eds., *Return.*

33. In interviews, UIC senior administrators told me that South Korean citizens made up at least three-quarters of each incoming class.

34. Students are classified as Overseas Korean if they are a South Korean citizen or have at least one parent with South Korean citizenship. They must also have completed at least three years of secondary education overseas.

35. The exemption of South Korean citizens who complete K–12 education overseas from the enrollment quotas set by the Ministry of Education is part of a broader effort by the South Korean government to repatriate South Korean citizens living abroad.

36. Ong, *Flexible Citizenship*, 134.

37. My earlier work focuses on the linguistic contradictions of UIC students as understood through a framework of Third Space. See Kim, "English Is for Dummies." See also Kim, "International College in South Korea as Third Space." Additionally, newer research reflects how South Korean students resist using English within English-only higher education settings. See Choi, " 'No English, Korean Only.' "

38. These figures are current as of Spring 2022. See Underwood International College, "Overview."

39. Jeon and An, "Is Underwood International College's Unique Identity Established?"; Kim, "Underwood International College Students Suffer."

4   The Contradictions of Choice

1. Abelmann, Choi, and Park, eds., *No Alternative?*

2. South Korean millennials are sometimes referred to as the "spec generation" because they are overly concerned with accumulating "specs," an abbreviated term for specifications that is intended to evoke a dystopian image of youth diminished to commercial products. See Cho, "Spec Generation Who Can't Say 'No.' "

3. Seth, *Education Fever.*

4. Park, "Educational Manager Mothers."

5. Abelmann, Park, and Kim, "College Rank and Neo-Liberal Subjectivity."

6. Hankuk Academy of Foreign Studies first opened in 2005 as a foreign language high school. However, since 2011, it has been designated as an independent private high school, which is another subcategory of special purpose high schools.

7. IIE, *Open Doors.*

8. KEDI, *Brief Statistics on Korean Education.*

9. OECD, *Education at a Glance.*

10. Jeff Selingo, *Who Gets in and Why.*

11. Jack, *Privileged Poor.*

12. Kim, "Voluntarily Exiled?"

13. Kim, "Voluntarily Exiled?"

14. In the 2010–2011 academic year, when Brandon would have first enrolled, nonresident tuition at the University of Colorado at Boulder was $28,000 per year.

15. Strayhorn, *College Students' Sense of Belonging*, 4.

16. Valenzuela, *Subtractive Schooling*.

17. Rizvi, "Towards Cosmopolitan Learning"; Waters, *Education, Migration, and Cultural Capital*.

18. Anagnost, Arai, and Ren, eds., *Global Futures in East Asia*, 2.

19. Ong, *Flexible Citizenship*; Ong, *Neoliberalism as Exception*.

20. Oh, "Escaping Obsolescence?"

21. University students in China also face the same uncertainties in their college admissions prospects. See Bregnbaek, *Fragile Elite*.

22. Lo and Kim, "Linguistic Competency and Citizenship"; Moon, *Militarized Modernity and Gendered Citizenship*; Choi and Chung, "Divergent Paths toward Militarized Citizenship."

23. Jung, "'I Know What Freedom and Responsibility Mean Now.'"

5   The Global Student Supply Chain

1. Xiang and Lindquist, "Migration Infrastructure."

2. Cranston, Schapendonk, and Spaan, "New Directions in Exploring the Migration Industries."

3. Shrestha and Yeoh, "Introduction."

4. Lindquist, Xiang, and Yeoh, "Opening the Black Box of Migration."

5. West, "Working with Agents."

6. West and Addington, *International Student Recruitment Agencies*.

7. NACAC, "Fact Sheet."

8. KOSA, *National Report for FELCA AGM*.

9. Collins, "Bridges to Learning."

10. UC Berkeley Extension is exempt from this policy and does indeed partner with agencies. In general, the UC system allows each campus to determine its own policy on education agents. For the UC-wide policy, see UCOP, "Undergraduate Recruitment Practices."

11. Nikula and Kivistö, "Hiring Education Agents."

12. Hamilton and Nielsen, *Broke*.

13. The popularity of intensive English programs may have waned among South Korean students. But education scholars Siyuan Feng and Hugo Horta show how they are still popular among Chinese students as part of a dual admissions strategy

into US colleges and universities. Furthermore, many Chinese students pursue this admissions strategy through the assistance of education agents. See Feng and Horta, "Brokers of International Student Mobility."

14. Dillon, "Elite Korean Schools"; Gamerman, "How to Get Into Harvard"; "The Rise of Korean Prep Schools."

15. Park, "Crafting and Dismantling the Egalitarian Social Contract."

16. KEDI, *Brief Statistics on Korean Education.*

17. Kang and Abelmann, "Domestication of South Korean Pre-College Study Abroad."

18. Kang and Abelmann, "Domestication of South Korean Early Study Abroad."

19. Kim and Kim, "Emerging High-Status Track."

20. As of 2021 there are thirty-four Korean International Schools operating across sixteen countries, most of which are located in East and Southeast Asia. See KEDI, *Brief Statistics.*

21. Brooks and Waters, "International Students and Alternative Visions."

22. The document was previously called the Code of Ethics and Professional Practices. Even prior to that, it was called the Statement of Principles of Good Practice.

23. For a full report on the investigations and hearings led by Congressman Sam Nunn, see U.S. Congress, *Abuses in Federal Student Aid Programs.*

24. McMillan Cottom, *Lower Ed.*

25. NACAC, *Guide to Ethical Practice in College Admission.*

26. For a full report on these debates, see NACAC, *Report of the Commission on International Student Recruitment.*

27. NACAC, *Guide to Ethical Practice.*

28. Shannon, *Losing Hearts and Minds.*

29. Yao and Mwangi, "Yellow Peril and Cash Cows."

30. Lee, ed., *U.S. Power in International Higher Education.*

31. U.S. Department of State and U.S. Department of Education, "Joint Statement of Principles in Support of International Education."

6   Lessons from a Turbulent Decade

1. Yang, *International Mobility and Educational Desire*; Xu, "Mainland Chinese Students at an Elite Hong Kong University."

2. Chen, "Impact of International Students on US Colleges."

Bibliography

AAC&U (Association of American Colleges and Universities). *What Liberal Education Looks Like.* Washington, DC: AAC&U, 2020.

Abelmann, Nancy. *The Intimate University: Korean American Students and the Problems of Self Segregation.* Durham, NC: Duke University Press, 2009.

Abelmann, Nancy, Jung-Ah Choi, and So Jin Park, eds. *No Alternative? Experiments in South Korean Education.* Oakland: University of California Press, 2012.

Abelmann, Nancy, So Jin Park, and Hyunhee Kim. "College Rank and Neo-Liberal Subjectivity in South Korea: The Burden of Self-Development." *Inter-Asia Cultural Studies* 10, no. 2 (2009): 229–247.

Alexander, Bryan. *Academia Next: The Futures of Higher Education.* Baltimore, MD: Johns Hopkins University Press, 2020.

Altbach, Philip G., and Jane Knight. "Internationalization of Higher Education: Motivations and Realities." *Journal of Studies in International Education* 11, no. 3/4 (2007): 290–305.

Anagnost, Ann, Andrea Arai, and Hai Ren, eds. *Global Futures in East Asia: Youth, Nation, and the New Economy in Uncertain Times.* Stanford, CA: Stanford University Press, 2013.

Appadurai, Arjun. *Modernity at Large: Cultural Dimensions of Globalization.* Minneapolis: University of Minnesota Press, 1996.

Apple, Michael W. *Education and Power*. 2nd ed. New York: Routledge, 1995.

Aronowitz, Stanley. *Against Schooling: For an Education That Matters*. New York: Routledge, 2008.

Arum, Richard, and Josipa Roska. *Academically Adrift: Limited Learning on College Campuses*. Chicago: University of Chicago Press, 2010.

Bady, Aaron, and Mike Konczal. "From Master Plan to No Plan: The Slow Death of Public Higher Education." *Dissent*, Fall 2012. https://www .dissentmagazine.org/article/from-master-plan-to-no-plan-the-slow-death-of -public-higher-education.

Beech, Suzanne. *The Geographies of International Student Mobility: Spaces, Places and Decision-Making*. London: Palgrave Macmillan, 2019.

Bleemer, Zachary. "Affirmative Action, Mismatch, and Economic Mobility after California's Proposition 209." *The Quarterly Journal of Economics* 137, no. 1 (2022): 115–160.

Bohn, Sarah, Belinda Reyes, and Hans Johnson. "The Impact of Budget Cuts on California's Community Colleges." San Francisco: Public Policy Institute of California, March 2013. https://www.ppic.org/publication/the-impact-of -budget-cuts-on-californias-community-colleges/.

Bok, Derek. *Our Underachieving Colleges: A Candid Look at How Much Students Learn and Why They Should Be Learning More*. Princeton, NJ: Princeton University Press, 2008.

Bowles, Samuel, and Herbert Gintis. *Schooling in Capitalist America: Educational Reform and the Contradictions of Economic Life*. New York: Basic Books, 1976.

Bregnbaek, Susan. *Fragile Elite: The Dilemmas of China's Top University Students*. Stanford, CA: Stanford University Press, 2016.

Brooks, Rachel, and Johanna Waters. "International Students and Alternative Visions of Diaspora." *British Journal of Educational Studies* 69, no. 5 (2021): 557–577.

Byun, Kiyong, and Minjung Kim. "Shifting Patterns of the Government's Policies for the Internationalization of Korean Higher Education." *Journal of Studies in International Education* 15, no. 5 (2010): 467–486.

Byun, Soo-yong. "Shadow Education and Academic Success in Republic of Korea." In *Korean Education in Changing Economic and Demographic Contexts*,

39–58. Education in the Asia-Pacific Region: Issues, Concerns and Prospects 23. Dordrecht, The Netherlands: Springer, 2014.

Cantwell, Brendan, and Ilkka Kauppinen, eds. *Academic Capitalism in the Age of Globalization*. Baltimore, MD: Johns Hopkins University Press, 2014.

Carnegie Classification of Institutions of Higher Education. *The Carnegie Classification of Institutions of Higher Education: 2018 Update Facts & Figures*. Bloomington, IN: Center for Postsecondary Research, 2019.

Chen, Kuan-Hsing. *Asia as Method: Toward Deimperialization*. Durham, NC: Duke University Press, 2010.

Chen, Mingyu. "The Impact of International Students on US Colleges: Higher Education as a Service Export," June 2021. https://ssrn.com/abstract=3859798.

Cheng, Yi'En. "Liberal Arts Educated Citizen: Experimentation, Subjectification, and Ambiguous Contours of Youth Citizenship." *Area* 51, no. 4 (2019): 618–626.

Cho, Hae-joang. "The Spec Generation Who Can't Say 'No': Overeducated and Underemployed Youth in Contemporary South Korea." *positions* 23, no. 3 (2015): 437–462.

Choi, Hee Jung, and Ga Young Chung. "Divergent Paths toward Militarized Citizenship: The 'Unending' Cold War, Transnational Space of Citizenship, and International Korean Male Students." *Korea Journal* 48, no. 3 (2018): 76–101.

Choi, Jinsook. "'No English, Korean Only': Local Students' Resistance to English as a Lingua Franca at an 'English Only' University in Korea." *Language and Intercultural Communication* 21, no. 2 (2021): 276–288.

Choudaha, Rahul. "Know Your International Student—Global or Glocal?" *University World News*, April 27, 2013. https://www.universityworldnews.com/post.php?story=20130426103907495.

Choudaha, Rahul. "A Third Wave of International Student Mobility." CSHE Research and Occasional Paper Series, CSHE.8.18. Berkeley, CA, April 2018.

Choudaha, Rahul, Kate Orosz, and Li Chang. "Not All International Students Are the Same: Understanding Segments, Mapping Behavior." World Education Services, August 1, 2012. https://wenr.wes.org/2012/08/wenr-feature-2012-not-all-international-students-are-the-same.

Chun, Jennifer Jihye, and Ju Hui Judy Han. "Language Travels and Global Aspirations of Korean Youth." *positions* 23, no. 3 (2015): 565–593.

Collins, Francis L. "Bridges to Learning: International Student Mobilities, Education Agencies and Inter-Personal Networks." *Global Networks* 8, no. 4 (2008): 398–417.

Collins, Francis L. *Global Asian City: Migration, Desire, and the Politics of Encounter in 21st Century Seoul.* Hoboken, NJ: Wiley-Blackwell, 2018.

Cook, Kevin. *Higher Education Funding in California.* San Francisco, CA: Public Policy Institute of California, March 2017. https://www.ppic.org /publication/higher-education-funding-in-california/.

Cranston, Sophie, Joris Schapendonk, and Ernst Spaan. "New Directions in Exploring the Migration Industries: Introduction to Special Issue." *Journal of Ethnic and Migration Studies* 44, no. 4 (2018): 543–557.

Dacin, M. Tina, Jerry Goodstein, and W. Richard Scott. "Institutional Theory and Institutional Change: Introduction to the Special Research Forum." *Academy of Management Journal* 45, no. 1 (2002): 45–57.

de Wit, Hans, Fiona Hunter, Laura Howard, and Eva Egron-Polak. *Internationalisation of Higher Education.* Brussels: European Parliament, 2015.

Deem, Rosemary, Ka Ho Mok, and Lisa Lucas. "Transforming Higher Education in Whose Image? Exploring the Concept of the 'World-Class' University in Europe and Asia." *Higher Education Policy* 21 (2008): 83–97.

Dillon, Sam. "Elite Korean Schools, Forging Ivy League Skills." *New York Times*, April 27, 2008.

DiMaggio, Paul J., and Walter W. Powell. "The Iron Cage Revisited: Institutional Isomorphism and Collective Rationality in Organizational Fields." *American Sociological Review* 48, no. 2 (1983): 147–160.

Douglass, John Aubrey. *The California Idea and American Higher Education: 1850 to the 1960 Master Plan.* Stanford, CA: Stanford University Press, 2000.

Douglass, John Aubrey. *The Conditions for Admission: Access, Equity, and the Social Contract of Public Universities.* Stanford, CA: Stanford University Press, 2007.

Douglass, John Aubrey. "The University of California Versus the SAT: A Brief History and Contemporary Critique." CSHE Research and Occasional Paper Series, CSHE.8.2020. Berkeley, CA, June 2020.

Eagleton, Terry. "The Slow Death of the University." *The Chronicle of Higher Education*, April 6, 2015.

Feng, Siyuan, and Hugo Horta. "Brokers of International Student Mobility: The Roles and Processes of Education Agents in China." *European Journal of Education Research, Development and Policy* 56, no. 2 (2021): 248–264.

Finch, John, and Seung-kyung Kim. "Kirŏgi Familes in the US: Transnational Migration and Education." *Journal of Ethnic and Migration Studies* 38, no. 3 (2012): 485–506.

Fischer, Karin, and Sasha Aslanian. "Fading Beacon: Why America Is Losing International Students." *APM Reports*, August 3, 2021. https://www.apmreports.org/episode/2021/08/03/fading-beacon-why-america-is-losing-international-students.

Fisher, Dara R. *Education Crossing Borders: How Singapore and MIT Created a New University*. Cambridge, MA: MIT Press, 2020.

Fong, Vanessa. *Paradise Redefined: Transnational Chinese Students and the Quest for Flexible Citizenship in the Developed World*. Stanford, CA: Stanford University Press, 2011.

Gamerman, Ellen. "How to Get into Harvard." *The Wall Street Journal*, November 30, 2007.

Gilmore, Janet. "In a Pandemic Year, UC Berkeley Admits Another Outstanding, More Diverse Class." *Berkeley News*, July 19, 2021. https://news.berkeley.edu/2021/07/19/in-a-pandemic-year-uc-berkeley-admits-another-outstanding-more-diverse-class/.

Hamilton, Laura T., and Kelly Nielsen. *Broke: The Racial Consequences of Underfunding Public Universities*. Chicago: University of Chicago Press, 2021.

Hazelkorn, Ellen. *Rankings and the Reshaping of Higher Education: The Battle for World-Class Excellence*. 2nd ed. New York: Palgrave Macmillan, 2015.

IIE (Institute of International Education). *Open Doors Report on International Educational Exchange*. Washington, DC: IIE, 2001–2021.

Immergut, Ellen M. "The Theoretical Core of the New Institutionalism." *Politics and Society* 26, no. 1 (1998): 5–34.

Jack, Anthony Abraham. *The Privileged Poor: How Elite Colleges Are Failing Disadvantaged Students*. Cambridge, MA: Harvard University Press, 2019.

Jaquette, Ozan, and Bradley R. Curs. "Creating the Out-of-State University: Do Public Universities Increase Nonresident Freshman Enrollment in Response to Declining State Appropriations?" *Research in Higher Education* 56 (2015): 535–565.

Jeon, Yehyeon (전예현), and An Hyogeun (안효근). "Is Underwood International College's Unique Identity Established? (언더우드국제대학만의 정체성, 확립 됐나)." *The Yonsei Chunchu*, November 5, 2017. http://chunchu.yonsei.ac.kr/news/articleView.html?idxno=23226.

Jiang, Shanshan. "Diversity Without Integration? Racialization and Spaces of Exclusion in International Higher Education." *British Journal of Sociology of Education* 42, no. 1 (2021): 32–47.

Jon, Jae-Eun. "Realizing Internationalization at Home in Korean Higher Education: Promoting Domestic Students' Interaction with International Students and Intercultural Competence." *Journal of Studies in International Education* 17, no. 4 (2013): 455–470.

Jung, Gowoon. "'I Know What Freedom and Responsibility Mean Now': Narratives of Autonomous Adulthood among Korean Students in the USA." *Young* 26, no. 4 (2018): 1–18.

Jung, Insung, Mikiko Ishimura, and Toshiaki Sasao. *Liberal Arts Education and Colleges in East Asia: Possibilities and Challenges in the Global Age.* Singapore: Springer, 2016.

Kang, Jiyeon, and Nancy Abelmann. "The Domestication of South Korean Early Study Abroad in the First Decade of the Millennium." In *South Korea's Education Exodus: The Life and Times of Study Abroad*, 40–60. Seattle: University of Washington Press, 2015.

Kang, Jiyeon, and Nancy Abelmann. "The Domestication of South Korean Pre-College Study Abroad in the First Decade of the Millennium." *Journal of Korean Studies* 17, no. 1 (2011): 89–118.

Kauppinen, Ilkka, Charles Mathies, and Lisa Weimer. "Developing a Conceptual Model to Study the International Student Market." In *Academic Capitalism in the Age of Globalization*, 246–264. Baltimore, MD: Johns Hopkins University Press, 2014.

KEDI (Korean Educational Development Institute). *Brief Statistics on Korean Education.* Jincheon, South Korea: KEDI, 2000–2021.

Kerr, Clark. *The Uses of the University*. Cambridge, MA: Harvard University Press, 1963.

Kim, Anna H., and Min-Jung Kwak, eds. *Outward and Upward Mobilities: International Students in Canada, Their Families, and Structuring Institutions*. Toronto: University of Toronto Press, 2019.

Kim, Doo Hwan, and Ji Hye Kim. "Emerging High-Status Track in South Korea: Social Capital Formation in the Social Contexts of Foreign Language and General High Schools." *Asia-Pacific Education Researcher* 22 (2013): 33–44.

Kim, Jaewon (김재원). "Underwood International College Students Suffer Due to Lack of Full-Time Professors (우리대학교 언더우드국제대학, 전임교수 부족으로 학생들 불편 겪는 것으로 나타나)." Yonsei Broadcasting System, November 8, 2017. https://www.youtube.com/watch?v=tN2A6ajipEw.

Kim, Stephanie K. "Coming to America: Reopening the United States to International Students." Washington, DC: Data Catalyst Institute, April 2021. https://datacatalyst.org/reports/reopening-america-to-international-students/.

Kim, Stephanie K. "English Is for Dummies: Linguistic Contradictions at an International College in South Korea." *Compare: A Journal of Comparative and International Education* 46, no. 1 (2016): 116–135.

Kim, Stephanie K. "Illegitimate Elites and the Politics of Belonging at a Korean University." *Journal of Korean Studies* 23, no. 1 (2018): 175–202.

Kim, Stephanie K. *An International College in South Korea as a Third Space between Korean and US Models of Higher Education*. University of California, 2014.

Kim, Stephanie K. "Western Faculty 'Flight Risk' at a Korean University and the Complexities of Internationalisation in Asian Higher Education." *Comparative Education* 52, no. 1 (2016): 78–90.

Kim, Sujung. "Voluntarily Exiled? Korean State's Cultural Politics of Young Adults' Social Belonging and Korean Students' Exile to a US Community College." *Higher Education* 76 (2018): 353–367.

Kim, Terri. "Academic Mobility, Transnational Identity Capital, and Stratification under Conditions of Academic Capitalism." *Higher Education* 73 (2017): 981–997.

Knight, Jane. "Internationalization Remodeled: Definition, Approaches, and Rationales." *Journal of Studies in International Education* 8, no. 1 (2004): 5–31.

KOSA (Korean Overseas Study Association). *National Report for FELCA AGM*. Seoul, South Korea: KOSA, 2011.

Lee, Hakyoon. "'I Am a Kirogi Mother': Education Exodus and Life Transformation among Korean Transnational Women." *Journal of Language, Identity, and Education* 9, no. 4 (2010): 250–264.

Lee, Jennifer, and Min Zhou. *The Asian American Achievement Paradox*. New York: Russell Sage Foundation, 2015.

Lee, Jenny J., ed. *U.S. Power in International Higher Education*. New Brunswick, NJ: Rutgers University Press, 2021.

Lee, Jenny J., and Charles Rice. "Welcome to America? International Student Perceptions of Discrimination." *Higher Education* 53 (2007): 381–409.

Lee, Tteulli (이뜰리). "Freshman and Transfer Students, the Unending Conflict (신입생과 편입생, 그 끝나지 않은 갈등)." *Berkeley Opinion*, November 8, 2015. https://berkeleyopinion.com/580.

Liu, Petrus, and Colleen Lye. "Liberal Arts for Asians: A Commentary on Yale-NUS." *Interventions* 18, no. 4 (2015): 573–587.

Lindquist, Johan, Bao Xiang, and Brenda S.A. Yeoh. "Opening the Black Box of Migration: Brokers, the Organization of Transnational Mobility and the Changing Political Economy of Asia." *Pacific Affairs* 85, no. 1 (2012): 7–19.

Lo, Adrienne, Nancy Abelmann, Soo Ah Kwon, and Sumi Okazaki. *South Korea's Education Exodus: The Life and Times of Study Abroad*. Seattle: University of Washington Press, 2015.

Lo, Adrienne, and Jenna Chi Kim. "Linguistic Competency and Citizenship: Contrasting Portraits of Multilingualism in the South Korean Popular Media." *Journal of Sociolinguistics* 16, no. 2 (2012): 255–276.

Looser, Tom. "The Global University, Area Studies and the World Citizen: Neoliberal Geography's Redistribution of the 'World." *Cultural Anthropology* 27, no. 1 (2012): 97–117.

Ma, Yingyi. *Ambitious and Anxious: How Chinese Students Succeed and Struggle in American Higher Education*. New York: Columbia University Press, 2020.

Marginson, Simon. *The Dream Is Over: The Crisis of Clark Kerr's California Idea of Higher Education.* Oakland: University of California Press, 2016.

Martin, Fran. *Dreams of Flight: The Lives of Chinese Women Students in the West.* Durham, NC: Duke University Press, 2022.

McMillan Cottom, Tressie. *Lower Ed: The Troubling Rise of For-Profit Colleges in the New Economy.* New York: The New Press, 2017.

Mo, Jongryn. *Korea's Quest for Global Education: The Underwood International College (UIC) Model.* Seoul: Global Education Forum, 2009.

Mohrman, Kathryn, Wanhua Ma, and David Baker. "The Research University in Transition: The Emerging Global Model." *Higher Education Policy* 21 (2008): 5–27.

Mok, Ka Ho. "Questing for Internationalization of Universities in Asia: Critical Reflections." *Journal of Studies in International Education* 11, no. 3/4 (2007): 433–454.

Moon, Rennie. "Internationalization without Cultural Diversity? Higher Education in Korea." *Comparative Education* 52, no. 1 (2016): 91–108.

Moon, Seungsook. *Militarized Modernity and Gendered Citizenship in South Korea.* Durham, NC: Duke University Press, 2005.

NACAC (National Association for College Admission Counseling). "Fact Sheet: Partnering with International Recruitment Agents During COVID." Arlington, VA: NACAC, 2021.

NACAC (National Association for College Admission Counseling). *Guide to Ethical Practice in College Admission.* Arlington, VA: NACAC, 2021.

NACAC (National Association for College Admission Counseling). *Report of the Commission on International Student Recruitment.* Arlington, VA: NACAC, 2013.

NAFSA: Association of International Educators. "The United States of America: Benefits from International Students." Washington, DC: NAFSA: Association of International Educators, 2020.

Newfield, Christopher. *The Great Mistake: How We Wrecked Public Universities and How We Can Fix Them.* Baltimore, MD: Johns Hopkins University Press, 2018.

Nikula, Pii-Tuulia, and Jussi Kivistö. "Hiring Education Agents for International Student Recruitment." *Higher Education Policy* 31 (2018): 535–557.

OECD (Organisation for Economic Co-operation and Development). *Education at a Glance: OECD Indicators*. Paris: OECD, 2021.

Oh, Hyun Joo S. "Escaping Obsolescence? The Shift from Subject to Skill Based Education in a South Korean International School." *Discourse: Studies in the Cultural Politics of Education* 39, no. 5 (2018): 814–828.

Ong, Aihwa. *Flexible Citizenship: The Cultural Logics of Transnationality*. Durham, NC: Duke University Press, 1999.

Ong, Aihwa. *Neoliberalism as Exception: Mutations in Citizenship and Sovereignty*. Durham, NC: Duke University Press, 2006.

Ortiga, Yasmin Y. *Emigration, Employability and Higher Education in the Philippines*. New York: Routledge, 2018.

Ortiga, Yasmin Y. "The Flexible University: Higher Education and the Global Production of Migrant Labor." *British Journal of Sociology of Education* 38, no. 4 (2017): 485–499.

Park, Joseph Sung-Yul, and Lionel Wee. *Markets of English: Linguistic Capital and Language Policy in a Globalizing World*. New York: Routledge, 2012.

Park, Julie J. *Race on Campus: Debunking Myths with Data*. Cambridge, MA: Harvard Education Press, 2018.

Park, Sang-Young. "Crafting and Dismantling the Egalitarian Social Contract: The Changing State-Society Relations in Globalizing Korea." *The Pacific Review* 23, no. 5 (2010): 579–601.

Park, So Jin. "Educational Manager Mothers: South Korea's Neoliberal Transformation." *Korea Journal* 47, no. 3 (2007): 186–213.

Park, So Jin, and Nancy Abelmann. "Class and Cosmopolitan Striving: Mothers' Management of English Education in South Korea." *Anthropological Quarterly* 77, no. 4 (2004): 645–672.

Phan, Le Ha. *Transnational Education Crossing "Asia" and "the West": Adjusted Desire, Transformative Mediocrity and Neo-Colonial Disguise*. New York: Routledge, 2017.

Poon, OiYan, and Megan S. Segoshi. "The Racial Mascot Speaks: A Critical Race Discourse Analysis of Asian Americans and Fisher vs. University of Texas." *The Review of Higher Education* 42, no. 1 (2018): 235–667.

Powell, Walter W., and Paul J. DiMaggio, eds. *The New Institutionalism in Organizational Analysis*. Chicago: University of Chicago Press, 1991.

Raby, Rosalind, Deborah Budd, Andrew Serban, and Dianne Van Hook. "International Student Mobility at California Community Colleges." In *Global Perspectives and Local Challenges Surrounding International Student Mobility*, 1–15. Hershey, PA: IGI Global, 2016.

"The Rise of Korean Prep Schools." *Newsweek*, August 8, 2008.

Rizvi, Fazal. "Towards Cosmopolitan Learning." *Discourse: Studies in the Cultural Politics of Education* 30, no. 3 (2009): 253–268.

Robertson, Shanthi, Yi'En Cheng, and Brenda S.A. Yeoh. "Introduction: Mobile Aspirations? Youth Im/Mobilities in the Asia-Pacific." *Journal of Intercultural Studies* 39, no. 6 (2018): 613–625.

Santa Monica College. "Tuition, Fees and Payment Deadlines," n.d. http://www.smc.edu/EnrollmentDevelopment/Admissions/Pages/Tuition-Fees.aspx.

Selingo, Jeff. *Who Gets in and Why: A Year Inside College Admissions*. New York: Scribner, 2020.

Seth, Michael. *Education Fever: Society, Politics, and the Pursuit of Schooling in South Korea*. Honolulu: University of Hawaii Press, 2002.

Shahjahan, Riyad A., and Adrianna J. Kezar. "Beyond the 'National Container': Addressing Methodological Nationalism in Higher Education Research." *Educational Researcher* 42, no. 1 (2013): 20–29.

Shannon, Matthew K. *Losing Hearts and Minds: American-Iranian Relations and International Education During the Cold War*. Ithaca, NY: Cornell University Press, 2017.

Shin, Gi-Wook. *Ethnic Nationalism in Korea: Genealogy, Politics, and Legacy*. Stanford, CA: Stanford University Press, 2006.

Shrestha, Tina, and Brenda S.A. Yeoh. "Introduction: Practices of Brokerage and the Making of Migration Infrastructures in Asia." *Pacific Affairs* 90, no. 4 (2018): 663–672.

Slaughter, Sheila, and Larry L. Leslie. *Academic Capitalism: Politics, Policies, and the Entrepreneurial University*. Baltimore, MD: Johns Hopkins University Press, 1999.

Slaughter, Sheila, and Gary Rhoades. *Academic Capitalism and the New Economy: Markets, State, and Higher Education*. Baltimore, MD: Johns Hopkins University Press, 2009.

Sohn, Minji. "A Ghost Story." Talk presented at the Dwelling In-Between: Korean Americans in the Bay Area, Berkeley, CA, October 21, 2017.

Springdale (스프링데일). "Transfer Students Who Wanted to Become Freshman Students (신입생이 되고 싶었던 편입생)." *Berkeley Opinion*, May 31, 2012. https://berkeleyopinion.com/216.

Strayhorn, Terrell L. *College Students' Sense of Belonging: A Key to Educational Success for All Students.* 2nd ed. New York: Routledge, 2019.

Stromquist, Nelly P. "Internationalization as a Response to Globalization: Radical Shifts in University Environments." *Higher Education* 53, no. 1 (2007): 81–105.

Thelin, John R. *A History of American Higher Education.* 3rd ed. Baltimore, MD: Johns Hopkins University Press, 2019.

UC Berkeley. "UC Berkeley Fall Enrollment Data," n.d. https://admissions .berkeley.edu/student-profile.

UCLA (University of California–Los Angeles). "Undergraduate Profile." Academic Planning and Budget, n.d. https://apb.ucla.edu/campus-statistics /undergraduate-profile.

UCOP (University of California Office of the President). "Admissions by Source School." UCOP, n.d. https://www.universityofcalifornia.edu/infocenter /admissions-source-school.

UCOP (University of California Office of the President). "Fall Enrollment at a Glance." UCOP, n.d. https://www.universityofcalifornia.edu/infocenter/fall -enrollment-glance.

UCOP (University of California Office of the President). "Major Features of the California Master Plan for Higher Education." Oakland, CA: UCOP, February 2017. https://www.ucop.edu/institutional-research-academic-planning /_files/California-master-pan-topic-brief.pdf.

UCOP (University of California Office of the President). "UC Board of Regents Approves Policy on Nonresident Student Enrollment." UCOP, May 18, 2017. https://www.universityofcalifornia.edu/press-room/uc-board-regents-approves -policy-nonresident-student-enrollment.

UCOP (University of California Office of the President). "Undergraduate Recruitment Practices." Oakland, CA: UCOP, December 18, 2014. https:// policy.ucop.edu/doc/2700628/UndergraduateRecruitmentPractices.

Underwood International College. "Overview." Yonsei University, n.d. https://uic.yonsei.ac.kr/main/about.asp?mid=m01_01_01.

Underwood International College. "Tuition Fee," n.d. https://uic.yonsei.ac.kr/main/admission.asp?mid=m04_03_01.

UNESCO Institute for Statistics. "Global Flow of Tertiary-Level Students," n.d. http://uis.unesco.org/en/uis-student-flow.

U.S. Congress. "Abuses in Federal Student Aid Programs." Permanent Subcommittee on Investigations of the Committee on Governmental Affairs. Washington, DC: Senate, 1991.

U.S. Department of State and U.S. Department of Education. "Joint Statement of Principles in Support of International Education." Washington, DC: EducationUSA, 2021.

Valenzuela, Angela. *Subtractive Schooling: U.S.–Mexican Youth and the Politics of Caring*. Albany, NY: SUNY Press, 1999.

Vavrus, Frances, and Lesley Bartlett, eds. *Critical Approaches to Comparative Education: Vertical Case Studies from Africa, Europe, the Middle East, and the Americas*. New York: Palgrave Macmillan, 2009.

Waters, Johanna L. *Education, Migration, and Cultural Capital in the Chinese Diaspora: Transnational Students Between Hong Kong and Canada*. Amherst, NY: Cambria Press, 2008.

Waters, Johanna, and Rachel Brooks. *Student Migrants and Contemporary Educational Mobilities*. London: Palgrave Macmillan, 2021.

Waters, Johanna, and Maggi Leung. "Immobile Transnationalisms? Young People and Their *in situ* Experiences of 'International' Education in Hong Kong." *Urban Studies* 50, no. 3 (2013): 606–620.

West, Eddie. "Working with Agents." *IEM Spotlight* 19, winter (2019). https://www.nafsa.org/professional-resources/browse-by-interest/working-with-agents.

West, Eddie, and Lindsay Addington. *International Student Recruitment Agencies: A Guide for Schools, Colleges and Universities*. Washington, DC: National Association for College Admission Counseling, 2014.

Wilbers, Stefan, and Jelena Brankovic. "The Emergence of University Rankings: A Historical-Sociological Account." *Higher Education* (2021). https://doi.org/10.1007/s10734-021-00776-7.

World Bank. "Fertility Rate, Total (Births per Woman)," 2021. https://data .worldbank.org/.

Xiang, Biao, and Johan Lindquist. "Migration Infrastructure." *International Migration Review* 48, no. S1 (2014): S122–148.

Xiang, Biao, Brenda S. A. Yeoh, and Mika Toyota, eds. *Return: Nationalizing Transnational Mobility in Asia.* Durham, NC: Duke University Press, 2013.

Xu, Cora Lingling. "Mainland Chinese Students at an Elite Hong Kong University: Habitus-Field Disjuncture in a Transborder Context." *British Journal of Sociology of Education* 38, no. 5 (2017): 610–624.

Yang, Peidong. *International Mobility and Educational Desire: Chinese Foreign Talent Students in Singapore.* New York: Palgrave Macmillan, 2016.

Yao, Christina W. "'They Don't Care About You': First-Year Chinese International Students' Experiences with Neo-Racism and Othering on a U.S. Campus." *Journal of the First-Year Experience and Students in Transition* 30, no. 1 (2018): 87–101.

Yao, Christina W., and Chrystal A. Mwangi. "Yellow Peril and Cash Cows: The Social Positioning of Asian International Students in the USA." *Higher Education*, 2022. https://doi.org/10.1007/s10734-022-00814-y.

Index

Page numbers in *italics* denote figures.

Abelmann, Nancy, 13
Academic capitalism, 8, 60–62
Admissions recruiters, 130–134, 154
Affirmative action, 38–39
Altbach, Philip, 8
Americanization, 31–32, 58, 59–62, 65–68, 163–164
Anti-Asian racism, 10, 23, 40–42
Appadurai, Arjun, 14
Aronowitz, Stanley, 60
Arum, Richard, 60
Asia as Method (Chen), 62
Asian American Achievement Paradox, The (Lee and Zhou), 39–40
Asian University for Women, 61
Association of American Colleges and Universities, 59–60
Audrey (UIC student), 69–70, 71–73, 81–84, 166–168

Bady, Aaron, 36–37
Bangladesh, 61
Bok, Derek, 60

Brain Korea 21 Project, 65
Brandon (UIC student), 108–113, 116
Broke (Hamilton and Nielsen), 129
Brooks, Rachel, 140
Bureau of Educational and Cultural Affairs, 148

California Civil Rights Initiative (1996), 38–39
California higher education. *See* Community college; University of California; University of California Berkeley (UC Berkeley)
California Master Plan for Higher Education, 7, 29–33
Capitalism, 8, 60–62. *See also* Globalization; Global student supply chain
Chen, Kuan-Hsing, *Asia as Method,* 62
Cheng, Yi'en, 15, 61
China
    Americanization of higher education in, 31–32, 61
    higher education reforms in, 163–164

China (cont.)
international student enrollment statistics, 13, *14*
racialized portrayals of COVID-19, 10
Cho, Kuk, 91
Choudaha, Rahul, 16
Class
admissions selectivity based on, 32
transnational vs. diasporic Koreans, 68–69
College of Liberal Studies (Seoul National University), 67
College Scholastic Ability Test (South Korean national college entrance exam), 88–90
Commodification of higher education, 6–11, 16–20, 147–148. *See also* Academic capitalism; Global student supply chain
Community college
gateway to the University of California, 18, 27–29, 45–48, *46*, 158
international recruitment strategies, 128–130
John (community college admissions recruiter), 130–134, 154
responses to reduced funding, 45–48, *46*
student experience: Jessica, 33–35, 42–45, 52–54, 55, 95, 164–166
student experience: Jihun, 27, 92–97, 114–115
student experience: Taeho, 103–108, 115–116
"transfer student" stigma, 48–54, 185n35
Cosmopolitanism, 13, 68–69
COVID-19 pandemic
conflicting international recruitment policies, 148
decreased international enrollment, 127

novel educational pathways and, 163–164
racialized rhetoric, 10, 23
Crazy Rich Asians (2018), 2

Daewon Foreign Language High School, 74, 134, 136
De Anza College, 47–48, 52–53, 128–130, 164–166
Diablo Valley College, 47–48, 92, 94–95, 128–130
Dissent magazine, 36–37
Domestic students, South Korea, 63–65, *64*, 73–77
Douglass, John Aubrey, 31, 32
Duke Kunshan University, 61

Eagleton, Terry, "The Slow Death of the University," 59
Early study abroad. *See also* International students
college admissions and, 90, 96, 97, 117, 160
downward trend in, 98
English fluency and, 12–13, 70–71, 97, 115, 117
foreign language high schools as extension of, 135–136
multigenerational transnationalism and, 93, 172
policies for transnational returnees, 93–94
student experiences of, 3, 12–13
UIC students and, 73, 74
Economics. *See also* Globalization; Great Recession (2007–2009)
Americanization as commercial enterprise, 67–68
commodification of higher education, 6–11, 16–20, 147–148
international enrollment and, 2–3, 13–16, *14, 16*, 63–65, *64*, 98

Education agents
  agency theory, 128
  Hyeonsuk (education agent), 124–127
  international recruitment agencies
    in South Korea, 122–124, 138–139,
    150–151, 154
  partnerships with colleges and universi-
    ties, 128–129, 132, 144
  professional associations and, 123
  regulatory policies around, 142–143,
    144–145, 148, 151–152
  rise of, 121–124
EducationUSA, 132, 133, 148–153, 155
*Emigration, Employability and Higher
  Education in the Philippines* (Ortiga),
  17
Ethnographic vignettes. *See* Industry
  experiences; Student experiences
Ethnography, institutional, 175–176,
  177
Ewha Womans University, 67

Federation of Education and Language
  Consultant Associations (FELCA),
  143
Flexible citizenship, 2, 113–117. *See also*
  Student choice
Flexible Citizenship (Ong), 2, 3
Flexible universities, 16–20
Foreign language high schools, 134–141,
  154–155
Foreignness, 77–80, 81–84, 109–111

Gayeong (foreign language high school
  teacher), 137–141
Globalization
  flexible universities within, 16–20
  inbound vs. outbound, 66
  internationalization of higher education
  and, 8–11
  South Korean approach to, 11–16, *16*,
  18–19

Global student supply chain
  acknowledging, 162
  community college recruitment,
    128–134, 154
  education agents, 121–127, 154
  EducationUSA, 132, 133, 148–153,
    155
  foreign language high schools, 134–141,
    154–155
  quasi-regulatory bodies, 141–146
  symbiotic ecosystem, 153–156
  United States policy, 9–10, 147–149,
    151, 152–153, 155
"Glocal" students, 16
Golden Age of American higher education, 7
Graduate School USA, 119–120, 141
Great Recession (2007–2009). *See also*
  Economics
  higher education budget cuts, 35–38,
    45–46, 60
  internationalization of higher educa-
    tion and, 6–11, *7*, *46*, 46–48
  student demographics and, 63–65, *64*
  student mobility and, 50, 98, 125

Hagwon (cram schools), 1, 63, 124
Hamilton, Laura, *Broke*, 129
Hankuk Academy of Foreign Studies, 97,
  187n6
Higher education. *See also* University of
  California Berkeley (UC Berkeley);
  Yonsei University
  college admissions process, South
    Korea, 89–92
  commodification of, 6–11, 16–20,
    147–148
  government disinvestment in, 35–38,
    45–46
  influence on student mobility, 5,
    16–20
  internationalization of, 8–9, 182n17

Higher Education Act (1992), 142, 148
Hybrid linguistic practices, 57, 73, 81,
    187n37
Hyeonsuk (education agent), 124–127

Immigration policies under Trump
    administration, 9, 147, 182n19
Inbound globalization, 66, 75
Industry experiences. *See also* Student
    experiences
  Gayeong (foreign language high school
    teacher), 137–141, 154–155
  Hyeonsuk (education agent), 124–127,
    154
  Jina (EducationUSA network), 148–153,
    155
  John (community college admissions
    recruiter), 130–134, 154
  Rob (quasi-regulatory bodies), 144–146,
    155
Institutional theory, 8–9
International admissions recruiters,
    130–134, 154
International colleges. *See* Underwood
    International College (UIC)
Internationalization
  Americanization, 31–32, 58, 59–62,
    65–68, 163–164
  definition of, 8–9, 182n17
  as economic response, 6–11, *7*, 17–19,
    64–65
  liberal arts education in Asia, 60–62
  South Korean approach to, 11–16, *16*,
    18–19
International Migration Review, 121
International students. *See also* Early
    study abroad
  contested influx of, 159–161
  enrollment statistics, 2–3, 13–16, *14*,
    16, *46*, 63–64, 98
  intraethnic tensions between, 1–2,
    48–52, 77–80, 160–161, 185n35

reconfigured, by UIC, 68–73
"rich international student" stereotype,
    1–4, 50–51, 80, 160
transnational returnees, 69–73,
    109–113
United States policy toward, 9–10,
    147–149, 152–153, 155

Japan, 61
Jeong, Changyeong, 66
Jessica (UC Berkeley student), 33–35,
    42–45, 52–54, 55, 95, 164–166
Jihun (community college student), 27,
    92–97, 114–115
Jina (EducationUSA network), 148–153,
    155
Jiyeong (South Korean parent), 170–173
John (community college admissions
    recruiter), 130–134, 154
Journal of Intercultural Studies, 15
Jung, Chang Young, 66

Katehi, Linda, 36
Kauppinen, Ilkka, 17
Kerr, Clark, 29
Kim, Young Sam, 15
Kivistö, Jussi, 128
Knight, Jane, 8, 9
Konczal, Mike, 36–37
Korea Advanced Institute of Science and
    Technology (KAIST), 15
Korea Overseas Study Association
    (KOSA), 123, 143, 151
Korea University, 67, 77

Language
  admissions requirements and, 47, 75,
    90–91, 134–137
  challenges to Korean linguistic ability,
    43, 68–69, 71, 100–101, 111–113
  early study abroad and, 12–13, 70–71,
    93, 97, 115, 117

English fluency as academic currency, 50–51, 71–72, 74–77, 79
hybrid linguistic practices, 57, 73, 81, 187n37
Latour, Bruno, 121
Lee, Jennifer, *The Asian American Achievement Paradox*, 39–40
Lee, Jenny, 41, 182n17
Leslie, Larry, 8
Liberal arts education, Americanization of, 59–62, 65–68, 163–164
Lindquist, Johan, 121
Lower Ed (McMillan Cottom), 142

Marginson, Simon, 31
Mathies, Charles, 17
McMillan Cottom, Tressie, *Lower Ed*, 142
Methodological nationalism, 4, 181n5
Migration infrastructure, 19, 121. *See also* Global student supply chain
Mo, Jongryn, 66

Napolitano, Janet, 6, 11
National Association of College Academic Counselors (NACAC), 141–142, 144–146, 151
Neo-racism, 41–42
Newfield, Christopher, 60
Nielsen, Kelly, *Broke*, 129
Nikula, Pii-Tuulia, 128
NYU Shanghai, 61

Ong, Aihwa, *Flexible Citizenship*, 2, 3
Ortiga, Yasmin, *Emigration, Employability and Higher Education in the Philippines*, 17
Outbound globalization, 66
Overseas Korean (admissions category), 70, 73, 140, 186n34

Park, Chung Hee, 89
Park, So Jin, 13

People's Initiative to Limit Property Taxation (1978), 37
Phan, Le Ha, *Transnational Education Crossing "Asia" and "the West"*, 62
Proposition 13 (1978), 37
Proposition 209 (1996), 38–39

Quasi-regulatory bodies, 141–146, 155

Race, admissions selectivity based on, 32
Racism
    intraethnic tensions between students, 1–2, 48–52, 77–80, 160–161, 185n35
    racialized admissions, 38–42
    racialized rhetoric around COVID-19, 10, 23
Regulations
    EducationUSA, 132, 133, 148–153
    quasi-regulatory bodies, 141–146, 155
    United States policy, 9–10, 147–149, 151, 152–153, 155
Rice, Charles, 41
"Rich international student" stereotype, 1–4, 50–51, 80, 160
Ritsumeikan Asia Pacific University, 61
Rob (quasi-regulatory work), 144–146
Robertson, Shanthi, 15
Roksa, Josipa, 60

Santa Monica College, 47, 105
School of Interdisciplinary Studies (Korea University), 67
Scranton College (Ewha Womans University), 67
Segyehwa drive, 15. *See also* Globalization: South Korean approach to
Selingo, Jeff, 105
Seoul, as oversaturated market, 150–151. *See also* Yonsei University
Seoul National University, 67
Seunghui (UIC student), 97–102, 115
Shin, Gi-Wook, 15

Shrestha, Tina, 121
Singapore, 61
Slaughter, Sheila, 8
"Slow Death of the University, The"
    (Eagleton), 59
Sohn, Minji, 11–12
Songdo, South Korea, 73
Sookmyung Kinder Academy, 170–173
Sora (UC Berkeley student), 1–2, 3, 19
South Korean higher education. *See also*
    Industry experiences; Student experi-
    ences; Yonsei University
    approach to internationalization,
        11–16, *16*, 18–19
    college admissions tracks, 88–92
    domestic student shortage, 63–65, *64*
    international colleges in, 57–59, 65–68
    international enrollment statistics,
        13–16, *14*, *16*, 63–65, *64*, 98
    liberal arts education and, 59, 62
Stakeholders. *See* Global student supply
    chain
Strayhorn, Terrell, 111
Stromquist, Nelly, 9
Student choice
    college admissions tracks, South Korea,
        88–92
    rethinking flexible citizenship, 113–117
    student experience: Brandon, 108–113,
        116
    student experience: Jihun, 27, 92–97,
        114–115
    student experience: Seunghui, 97–102,
        115
    student experience: Taeho, 103–108,
        115–116
Student demonstrations, 35–38, 80
Student experiences. *See also* Industry
    experiences
    Audrey (UIC student), 69–70, 71–73,
        81–84, 166–168
    Brandon (UIC student), 108–113, 116

    of early study abroad, 12–13
    Jessica (UC Berkeley student), 33–35,
        42–45, 52–54, 55, 95, 164–166
    Jihun (community college student), 27,
        92–97, 114–115
    Seunghui (UIC student), 97–102, 115
    Taeho (UC Berkeley student), 103–108,
        115–116
    Yuri (UIC student), 74–76, 77, 81–84,
        168–170
Student mobility. *See also* Early study
    abroad; Globalization; Global student
    supply chain; International students;
    Student choice; University of Cali-
    fornia Berkeley (UC Berkeley); Yonsei
    University
    acknowledging global student supply
        chain, 162
    emergence of novel pathways, 158–159
    future of, 170–173
    institutional influence on, 5, 16–20,
        150, 162
    post-COVID-19 pandemic, 163–164
Student recruitment. *See also* Education
    agents
    community college recruitment,
        128–134
    conflicting policies around COVID-19,
        148
    ethics in, 125–127, 131, 141–143,
        144–146, 151, 156
    United States policy, 9–10, 147–149,
        151, 152–153, 155
Study Korea Project, 64–65
Subtractive schooling, 111
Suneung (South Korean national college
    entrance exam), 88–90

Taeho (UC Berkeley student), 103–108,
    115–116
Thelin, John, 7
Third Space theory, 81

"Transfer student" stigma, 48–54, 185n35

Transnational Education Crossing "Asia" and "the West" (Phan), 62

Transnational returnees. *See* Audrey (UIC student); Brandon (UIC student)

Transnational vs. diasporic Koreans, 68–69

Trump administration, 9–10, 21–22, 147–148, 153

Underwood, Horace Grant, 66

Underwood International College (UIC). *See also* Yonsei University
as contentious learning space, 77–80, 161
establishment of, 57–59, 65–68, 158–159
hybrid linguistic practices, 57, 73, 81, 187n37
reconfiguring domestic students, 73–77
reconfiguring international students, 68–73
student experience: Audrey, 69–70, 71–73, 81–84, 166–168
student experience: Brandon, 108–113, 116
student experience: Seunghui, 97–102, 115
student experience: Yuri, 74–76, 77, 81–84, 168–170

United States Department of State, 120, 148–149, 151

United States higher education. *See also* Community college; University of California; University of California Berkeley (UC Berkeley)
Americanization, 31–32, 58, 59–62, 65–68, 163–164
EducationUSA, 132, 133, 148–153, 155

immigration and international recruitment policy, 9–10, 147–149, 152–153

"Trump effect," 21–22, 163

University of California, 6–7, *7*, 11, 38–42

University of California Berkeley (UC Berkeley). *See also* Yonsei University
California Master Plan and, 29–33
community college transfer system, 27–29, 45–48, *46*
"freshman" vs. "transfer" students, 48–52, 185n35
higher education budget cuts and, 35–38
student experience: Jessica, 33–35, 42–45, 52–54, 55, 95, 164–166
student experience: Jihun, 27, 92–97, 114–115
student experience: Sora, 1–2, 3, 19
student experience: Taeho, 103–108, 115–116

University of California Davis, 36, 38

Uses of the University, The (Kerr), 29

Wallace, Alexandra, 40

Waters, Johanna, 113, 140

Weimer, Leasa, 17

Women, responsibility for children's success, 96

World Class University Project, 65

World Trade Organization, 8

Xenophobia
COVID-19 pandemic and, 10, 23
domestic pushback and, 54–55
racialized admissions, 38–42

Xiang, Biao, 121

Yale-NUS College, 61

Yeoh, Brenda, 15, 121

Yeongju (South Korean parent), 92, 94, 96

Yonsei University. *See also* University of
    California Berkeley (UC Berkeley)
    American liberal arts model, 59–62
    as contentious learning space, 77–80,
        161
    domestic student quotas and, 68, 70,
        158
    establishment of UIC, 57–59, 65–68,
        158–159
    reconfiguring domestic students, 73–77
    reconfiguring international students,
        68–73
    student experience: Audrey, 69–70,
        71–73, 81–84, 166–168
    student experience: Brandon, 108–113
    student experience: Seunghui, 97–102,
        115
    student experience: Yuri, 74–76, 77,
        81–84, 168–170
Yuhagwon (international recruitment
    agencies). *See* Education agents
Yuri (UIC student), 74–76, 77, 81–84,
    168–170

Zhou, Min, *The Asian American Achieve-
    ment Paradox*, 39–40